GARDEN
SURFACES

20 projects for

steps
patios
paths
decks
edging

RICHARD KEY

LAUREL
GLEN

San Diego, California

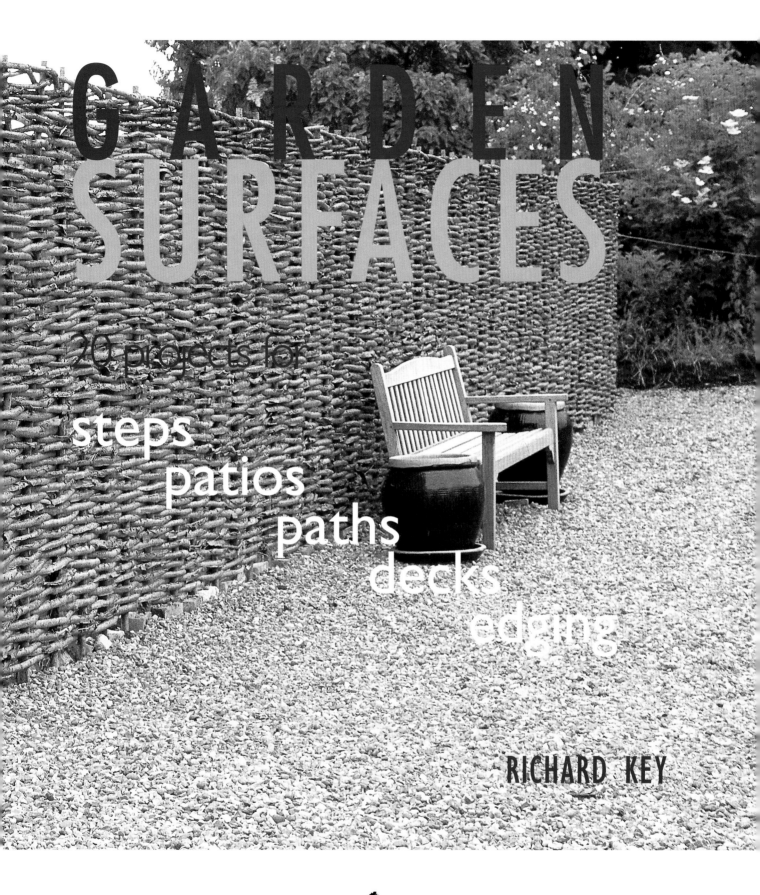

GARDEN
SURFACES

20 projects for

steps

patios

paths

decks

edging

RICHARD KEY

LAUREL
GLEN

San Diego, California

contents

planning a garden landscape

your GARDEN LANDSCAPE

A good, sound design is essential in achieving a well-balanced and harmonious garden with all elements in proportion. It is important to consider the layout of the whole garden, especially if it is a fairly small plot and every part of it will be visible at any one time. This book will show you how to plan and execute your ideas to create the perfect garden landscape.

A well-planned garden results in harmony between all its elements.

Once you have decided that you want to make changes to your garden space, you need to determine how your plans for any new projects can be incorporated into the existing garden. Their shape, size, and finished level are all important considerations, as well as how they blend in with what is already there.

A clear plan should be developed at this early stage because without one, it is all too easy to fall into the trap of piecemeal construction. This book will lead you through each of the stages of garden planning and construction, providing you with helpful advice and explanations so that you can create a well-balanced, easy-to-maintain garden to suit your own needs. Use it to ensure success in your garden.

Using this book

All the important stages of planning, constructing, and maintaining your garden surfaces are covered by this highly informative book. This first section describes the basics of planning a good garden design, from listing all your requirements to surveying the plot and then putting your ideas down on paper.

Time spent on thorough design work will ensure that the overall appearance is good and in harmony with the surroundings, that everything is in proportion, and that the whole space works. Invariably, if it looks right on paper, it will look right on the ground. Planning does not stop when the design is drawn up though, because you will need to plan the construction time and materials carefully. You cannot just go straight out and build a patio, for example, without planning how long it will take and exactly what materials are needed in order to construct it.

The other main ingredient in the creation of successful garden surfaces is a sound knowledge of construction techniques, not only so that the paving looks good, but also so that it is safe and will be long lasting. The section on techniques runs through all the practical stages, from marking out the site to the finishing touches.

The book then describes twenty practical and inspirational projects that illustrate different styles of construction for all types of garden surfaces. The subjects covered by these projects include pathways, edgings, steps, and patios.

The details of how to complete each project are given using clear, step-by-step photography and accompanying text. Any alternative materials or methods that can be employed are also indicated in order to provide you with additional ideas on how to tailor a specific project to your own garden space.

All-important advice on how to maintain your new garden surfaces, as well as the tools you will need to create them, is given at the end.

Before you begin

To aid you with the planning stage, there are several checklists that need to be drawn up, which will help you to assess all your requirements for the garden. This may cover more than you need for your particular construction projects, but it is best to look at the larger picture to ensure that everything will fit together in the end. For example, you need to think about what you will use the space for, what existing features you wish to keep, and any budget restraints you may have. From the lists that you draw up, you will then be able to pull out the information relevant for your construction projects.

Your basic requirements

It is important to spend time looking at your garden while thinking about what you want to use the space for. You should also determine what landscaping needs to be done and what existing construction needs to be worked into your new design. The following two lists show the sorts of things you should be considering when you draw up your initial plans.

Front garden

• Is there clear access to the front door, or do you need to create a new pathway?
• Is there an incline, and if so, are steps or a slope preferable?
• Is a parking space needed, and how much space is needed?
• What existing features do you wish to keep?
• Is there space to use the front garden for other purposes? (For a large front plot, also consider the requirements that are listed here for the rear garden.)

Rear garden

• What do all the members of the family require from the garden: do you need to satisfy an enthusiastic gardener, use the garden for relaxation and entertaining, or provide play areas for children?
• Where are the most suitable places for seating, given the direction of the sun and other features such as boundaries and trees?
• How many people should the sitting areas be planned for, and how much space will be needed?
• Which areas of the garden need to be accessed for gardening, playing, hanging clothes to dry, or storage, and will these be best served with paths, lawns, or steps?
• What are the best positions for these thoroughfares, both functionally and visually?
• Are edges or mowing strips required in the garden at all?
• What existing features do you wish to keep?

Budgetary requirements

In addition to this information, you will also have to consider your budget for the construction work. If you are doing all the work yourself, you will only need to plan the cost of materials and tool rental.

Choose the best surface material you can afford, but compromises can be made to fit in with your budget without spoiling the job. For instance, you could choose a good imitation of natural stone instead of the real thing. You could also spread construction projects over a couple of years, which would also cut the immediate cost. As long as you plan carefully, it can be helpful to construct your garden over different years and seasons.

You may also consider using a professional garden designer who will be trained in maximizing the potential of your garden, thereby saving you a lot of time and possible heartache. Many countries have an organization of garden designers that can supply you with a list of designers who will be able to help you with planning, establishing budgets, and will also be able to recommend contractors if you need help with construction work.

Existing site conditions

There is one final checklist to produce before embarking on your site survey: a list of existing site conditions that can be marked onto your survey drawing.

• Use a compass point to determine the positions of different features in your garden.
• Use a pH kit to check the soil's acidity and alkalinity. This will help you determine which plants will grow best. Sand and clay content will indicate how well-drained the soil is and how much excavated soil will bulk up.
• Make a note of garden features you need to remove, such as an old shed.
• Mark where there are wet corners (to drain or plant with bog plants) and shady corners (to create areas for cool seating).
• Note any underground pipes.
• Mark any existing trees (their height and canopy spread), any trees from adjacent gardens that cast a shadow in yours, and existing plantings—both good and bad.
• Your survey should show house walls, fences, and existing paving.
• Take photographs showing both good and bad views of the garden to help with your planning.

surveying AND PLANNING

One of the most important aspects of garden design is taking time to plan carefully on paper before beginning any of the physical work. Taking a survey of your garden so that you can make a detailed, scaled plan will help you enormously when you actually carry out the job.

Taking measurements

Make a simple sketch plan (not to scale) on a pad to show the house, the boundaries, and any existing features, such as trees or a shed. Then fix a tape measure to the side of the house and pull it out along the outside—start from one corner, at zero, and record a series of running measurements to show window and door positions. Add the measurements to your sketch. This process can then be repeated for all sides of the house.

The corners of the garden can be fixed by triangulation, which involves taking measurements from two points on the house to each corner of the garden. To do this, you can either use a long tape pulled out from the house to each corner, or walk between the two points using a measuring wheel. Triangulation can also be used to fix the position of trees or drain covers in the middle of the garden. Measure along each boundary using running measurements to record the position of gates or any significant plantings.

Survey drawing

Do a survey drawing to mark the existing features of your plot.

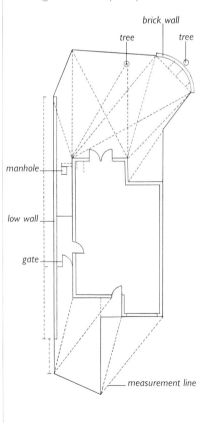

brick wall
tree   tree
manhole
low wall
gate
measurement line

Recording levels

Even if your garden appears to be flat, it may not be. A small slope can be measured by holding a straightedge and a level (also known as a "spirit level") out from the top of the slope and measuring down from the underside of the straightedge to the bottom. This is not practical for a whole garden; here it would be best to use a laser level (see page 21). In a small garden, you will only need to record a couple of levels adjacent to the house and the levels at each corner of the back boundary. A difference between the readings will indicate a slope, but if the readings are all equal, then the ground is level. Take another reading on a fixed point so it won't be disturbed, such as the insulation in the house wall.

Using a measuring wheel.

Use a laser level to measure the gradient.

Starting to plan

When your survey is complete, you can draw up a plan to scale on a clean sheet of paper. Most small to medium gardens can be drawn up to a scale of 1:50 or ¾ in.:40 in., so you will not need a massive sheet of paper.

Start by drawing the outline of your house using a scale ruler to mark the running measurements that you have taken along each wall. Then fix all the corners of the plot onto paper using a pair of compasses. Mark onto the plan an arc line for each of the triangulation measurements—where the arc lines meet will be the correct position in each case.

Now start to plan the detail of your garden. Use tracing paper laid over the top of your plan. This will enable you to make alterations on the overlay without spoiling the plan drawing underneath.

Ideas for the garden, including patios, lawns, etc., can be drawn up as a series of overlays on the plan. While you are doing each of these sketch overlays, you should start looking at the proposed areas in greater detail. For example, make sure that the pathways that link the different parts of the garden are wide enough, even with plants tumbling over the edges to soften the overall effect. Look carefully at the existing site levels and begin to determine what size treads and risers you will need for any connecting steps. Try to look beyond the existing features and search for imaginative and practical solutions.

When you are satisfied that the right design has been reached, place a fresh piece of tracing paper on top of your series of overlays and transfer the complete outline plan onto it (see illustration, right).

Drawing a plan to scale

An outline plan of your garden can be drawn to show proposed areas of different hard and soft landscaping features.

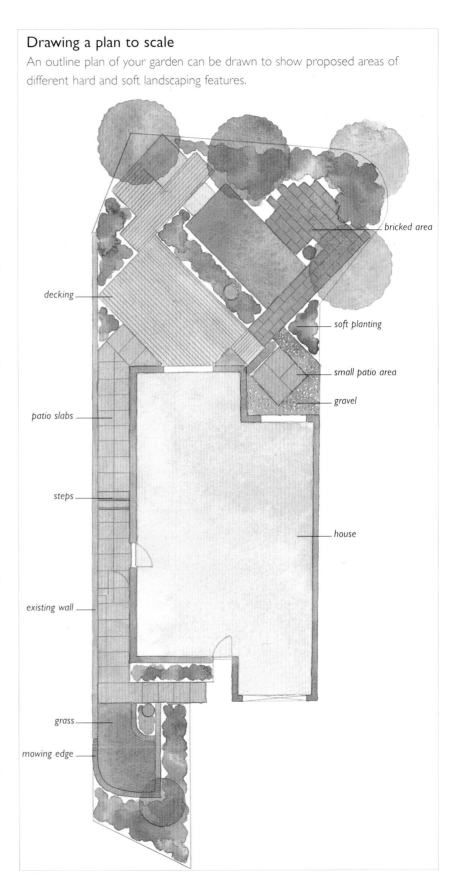

bricked area

soft planting

small patio area

gravel

decking

patio slabs

steps

house

existing wall

grass

mowing edge

surface DETAIL

It is important to think carefully about the surface color and texture when planning your garden landscape, because these decisions can have a significant impact on the finished result. For example, a blue slate path would look dramatic in a contemporary setting, while a patio made out of granite setts would be more suited to a traditional, natural-style garden.

Points to consider

There is a wide choice of materials available and a variety of patterns possible for garden surfaces, but before you begin buying your paving, consider a variety of factors that will influence your choice: function, location, style, and cost.

Function

Consider the function of your garden surface. Paving for a utility area should be hard wearing, but it does not need to be decorative. Secondhand paving slabs would be ideal for areas around a shed or compost bins. Stepping-stones are fine if used only occasionally, whereas hard-wearing bricks would be more suitable for a path that is used frequently. Bricks could also be used to form steps with narrow treads for quick access, while broad treads, perhaps in gravel, with a timber riser, could be constructed for a more leisurely ascent.

Location

The location of your proposed patio or path site is important. A natural stone terrace in full sun would be wonderful, but the same material in the shade of trees could become slippery and dangerous. The same thing applies to decking, which also needs to be sited in a sunny location

to keep the surface from becoming treacherous—rough-surfaced bricks or gravel will give a better grip for paving and paths in shady areas. The area around a swimming pool will also require a surface that can cope with regular splashing without becoming slippery—brushed concrete, textured bricks, or concrete paving slabs would all be suitable.

Style

The type of house, the local materials, and the proposed style of the garden will all affect your choice of paving materials. Where possible, try to use indigenous materials for hard landscaping, because sandstone paving, for example, may look somewhat incongruous in an area where slate is the native rock. Try to make sure that the materials that you choose are in keeping with the style of the garden. Brick paths will look right in a cottage garden, whereas concrete and stained decking probably would not.

Cost

Remember that the same effect can be achieved with more than one type of material of varying cost. For example, natural stone is expensive, but there are some good imitations in concrete, which are cheaper.

Choice of materials

There is a wide choice of paving materials available today, not just in garden centers, but also from stone suppliers, brick manufacturers, builders' merchants, and salvage yards. Also consider using the materials listed below in combination with one another.

Natural stone

Sandstone is probably the most suitable stone for garden paving. It has a warm color that mellows with age, and it blends well with brick, timber, gravel, and plants. Limestone is usually too soft to be used as paving, but slate on the other hand is a very dense, hard-wearing material that looks terrific in crisp, geometric designs.

Natural slate.

Precast concrete slabs

There are many types to choose from in all colors, shapes, and sizes. The subdued stone colors look better in the garden than more gaudy varieties. Textured slabs are excellent for a non-slip surface and look great laid in bands. Imitation stone slabs are also available.

Precast concrete slabs with bricks.

Setts

Setts are widely available either as sandstone or granite blocks. Alternatively, there are some cheaper setts made from concrete that are very good. They are all hard-wearing and are ideal for making step treads and curved paths.

Granite setts.

Gravel

Loose aggregate, such as gravel, is an excellent material available as crushed stone or small, smooth stones from gravel pits. The size of gravel for surfacing ranges from $^3/_8$–$^3/_4$ in. and the depth of the surface needs to be about $^3/_4$ in.

Loose aggregate.

Bricks

Choose clay rather than concrete bricks, as their soft colors are more suited to a garden. They work well for straight or curved paths, as a trim to other paving, or in patterns, such as running bond, basket weave, and herringbone.

Bricks in basket-weave pattern.

Cobblestones and pebbles

These are smooth, round stones ranging from $^3/_4$–4 in., which can be laid loose for a beach effect or bedded in mortar for a pathway. They can make intricate mosaic patterns and are often bordered by bricks or tiles.

Cobblestone and slate mosaic.

Timber

Wood is a versatile material that looks good in informal settings. Wood rounds can be laid for stepping-stones, wood chips can be used to dress up a pathway, and timber decking forms a superb sitting area in a sunny site.

Stained timber decking.

planning AND ESTIMATING

Carrying out garden construction requires considerable planning. You cannot roll out of bed on a Saturday morning without any preparation and expect to achieve anything worthwhile. Even if the project is a small one, there may be as much organization needed as for larger jobs: the same tools, safety checks, and visits to supply stores will be needed.

Planning construction work

If there are several projects planned, it is important that they are built in the correct order. There is no point in constructing a beautiful brick path only to trek along it with wheelbarrows and mixers to build a patio farther down the garden at some later stage. Either build the patio first, or better still, lay a path of compacted gravel to provide firm access and then lay the surface of bricks once the patio has been completed.

The beauty of preparing a landscape plan for the whole garden is that this allows you to plan the work in the right order. All the leveling and excavation work can be done at one time, even if the finished surfaces for different areas are to be laid over a period of time. This is not only economical, as it avoids the costs of bringing a machine back to your garden again, but it also avoids the risk of the machine damaging the newly laid paving.

Working to an overall plan also allows you to build individual areas to suit your budget with the knowledge that the area will be at the correct finished level. Without a plan, paved areas are often built in a piecemeal fashion, in total isolation from each other, which results in some very odd, often dangerous, changes in the level of the garden to connect them to each other. Your garden will look much more unified if you have spent time planning it out first.

Transporting materials along a gravel path.

Estimating time

Once you have decided on the correct order of operations, you will need to plan your time to carry out the work. Unless you have some prior knowledge of construction work, you will find the greatest danger is underestimating just how long a job will actually take. It is not a good idea to plan the construction of a patio on a Saturday and expect it to be finished for use for a party on Sunday. Depending on the skill involved in an operation, you may find that a day's work for a professional will be closer to five days for an amateur. You should certainly plan to double your initial time estimates, as there are unforeseen factors that can cause delays—notably bad weather or the possibility of machine breaking down.

Also, remember that you cannot work until dark, because you will need to allow an hour of daylight for cleaning tools and mixers. Bear in mind that if you can only work on the garden during weekends, everything must be packed away for the week, and rented machines must be returned to the store. So allow plenty of time when you do your estimate, and you might get to enjoy the feeling of finishing a day early.

Estimating materials

In addition to estimating time, you will also need to estimate the quantities of

Use your plan to calculate how many slabs you need.

materials required for the job. This can be quite tricky, and if you have any doubts, ask for advice from a reputable supply store. Unit materials

Calculating how many bricks you will need.

such as paving slabs can easily be estimated from the plan.

To save counting all the bricks for a pathway, simply calculate how many are needed for one square yard and then multiply that number by the total area in square yards of the path. If the bricks are to be laid flat with mortar joints, you will need thirty-three per square yard while, if they are laid on their edge with mortar joints, you will need fifty per square yard. It is a good idea to add an extra five percent to your estimates for all surfacing materials to allow for breakage.

Loose materials such as sand and gravel may be sold by volume in cubic yards and are straightforward to estimate by simply multiplying the area by the depth. It can be more confusing when these same materials are sold by weight in tons (cwt), as one cubic yard of sand will not weigh the same as one cubic yard of gravel. Where materials are sold by weight, ask the supplier to assist you with calculating how this equates to cubic yards.

Mortar may be sold dry in bags, requiring only the addition of water. This is ideal for small jobs, because it is easy to buy a few extra bags if you

Gravel is sold by volume.

discover that you need them. For larger areas of construction, it is more economical to buy sand in bulk, along with individual bags of cement. Of

Making mortar
Approximately 1 ton
(20 cwt) of mortar is needed to fill
$\frac{2}{3}$ cubic yd. (see page 26).
In the example below, the mortar mix is 1:6, one part cement to six parts sand (a total of seven parts), but this formula can be applied to different mortar mixes in order to calculate the amount of sand and cement required.

1 ton (20 cwt) of mortar covers
$\frac{2}{3}$ cubic yd.
1 part cement: 6 parts sand
= 7 parts in total.
1 ton (20cwt)÷7 = 3 cwt
for 1 part.
3 cwt cement : 17 cwt of sand.
Therefore, allowing for waste,
you will need six $\frac{1}{2}$-cwt bags of cement and 1 ton of sand to make
1 ton (20 cwt) of mortar.

course, it is important to know how much sand and cement you need to make up a quantity of mortar, and again you could seek advice from your supplier. However, the "Making mortar" box (below left) may serve as a useful guide and will also help with your initial cost estimate.

Obviously, the more construction work you carry out, the more knowledge you will gain. You will see that gravel may compact down by approximately ten to fifteen percent of its volume, while excavated soil may bulk up by twenty-five percent or more. Both these factors will need to be accounted for when ordering gravel and a wheelbarrow for the removal of soil. As you become more experienced, you will also become more accurate and confident at estimating the materials that you need for a job.

Ordering materials
Order all your materials well in advance of when you will need them, because you cannot always expect delivery the next day. You may get lucky, but most suppliers require at least two days' notice to deliver stock items. If possible, try to arrange for all your materials to be delivered in one load, as this will save on delivery costs.

Machinery and any specialty tools can be rented by the day or the week. They will also need to be ordered in advance so that you can be sure of getting them in time. If you are unfamiliar with any of the equipment you want to use, the supplier will almost always provide a demonstration and guide you through all the necessary safety procedures.

tools and techniques

preparing THE PLOT

Once you have a completed plan, you will need to transfer the measurements for the new paved areas from the plan onto the ground. To mark out the features on the whole site would be too confusing, so simply mark out the area of paving you are ready to build. You may find that you have to remove some unwanted plants before you can begin construction.

Marking out a rectangular area

1 First establish a baseline from which all other measurements can be taken. You can use the triangulation method for this (see page 10). For a rectangular area away from the house, fix two points: one at each end of one of the sides of the area. Drive a peg in at each point and join together with a string line to form the baseline.

2 Mark out the other sides at right angles to the baseline. Make a large wooden right-angled triangle with sides in the ratio of 3:4:5 to form a perfect right angle. Set one of the short sides of the triangle against the baseline and pull a string out taut along the other short side. The line, tied around a peg, will be at a right angle to the baseline.

3 Repeat this for the other side and join the two pegs with string to complete the shape. Finally, check that the diagonals are equal.

4 Sprinkle sand or spray marker paint along the string line to show the outline of the area on the ground.

5 Remove the string to allow for excavation, but leave them attached to the pegs so they can easily be put up again when construction work starts. Alternatively, you could set the pegs just outside the area of excavation.

Marking out a circular area

1 On your plan, use the triangulation method and draw a line from two points on the house wall (or from the boundaries, if closer) to meet in the center of your patio. To transfer this information onto the ground, use two long tape measures from the two fixed points, pull the tapes out taut to the measurements shown on the plan, and bring them together to fix the position of the center of the circle.

2 Drive a peg in at the center point, tie a string line around it, and then measure along that line to the correct radius of the circular paved area.

3 Tie a pointed stick or screwdriver to the line at this measurement and scratch out a circle on the ground with the string pulled taut. On lawn areas, you may have to scratch deeply through the turf so that the line can be seen. Mark the scratch line with sand

or paint for extra clarity, as shown for the rectangular area (Step 4).

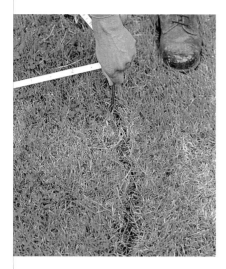

Marking out a curved path

Curved lines for pathways must be accurately marked out, so do not be tempted just to lay a garden hose on the ground as a guide. You need to measure the curve out precisely.

1 First, draw your proposed curved lines onto your plan. Then measure a series of offsets—lines that are measured at 90° from a baseline to points at regular intervals along the curved line—and note their lengths on the plan.

2 Next, measure and transfer the offsets onto the ground. First, transfer where your baseline should be from the plan. Next, measure out from that line at the same intervals and distances as shown on your scaled plan, to fix the points for the curve.

3 You will need a long tape to run along the baseline and a second tape to measure the offsets. A 3:4:5 triangle will ensure that the offsets are at 90° to the baseline. You can then drive a timber peg into the ground at the end

of each offset to fix these points for reference purposes.

4 Run a line of sand from one peg to the next to indicate the proposed curved line. For a straight path, establish one edge as the baseline and measure offsets out from each end that are equal to the width of the path to indicate the other path edge.

Ground clearance

You may need to do some initial clearance work before you are able to mark out the site with any accuracy. Remove all trash, bricks, concrete, and unwanted plant material, and cut down any long grass because it is

impossible to mark out accurately on this surface. All vegetation will need to be removed from areas to be excavated, and although short grass will rot down quickly, an application of weed killer (be sure to follow the manufacturer's instructions carefully) will certainly help the process.

Areas of paving should not be laid over loose soil or soft ground, so any topsoil must be removed down to firm ground. If paving is laid on top of loose ground, there is a high risk that the ground will settle and cause the paving to subside and crack.

However, topsoil is a valuable commodity, so if it can be used elsewhere in the garden to form levels in beds or elsewhere, set it aside. If you cannot use the extra topsoil, then do not bother placing it to one side; simply excavate straight down to the correct level and remove all the excavated material from the site.

Avoid the temptation to pave over the old patio and pathways, as this is rarely successful. New paving that has been placed over existing surfaces may bring the paved area too close to the insulating layer, which could then let wetness into the house. In addition, the levels of the old paving may be incorrect or may not allow for adequate drainage of the new surface. Perhaps more important, you will not be able to inspect the base under the old paving, which may be totally insufficient and will undoubtedly cause the new paving to settle and crack after a short period of time.

When planning new construction work, the best approach is simply to clear out all old constructions and start afresh with the correct depth of base material.

setting OUT LEVELS

Before beginning any construction work, you need to establish the proposed finished levels of your paving in relation to the surrounding, existing ground level. Using fairly simple or more sophisticated equipment, there are various methods of measuring the levels and marking them out on your new site, all of which are described below.

Planning

The existing levels of your garden will have been recorded when the garden was surveyed (see page 10). This survey should indicate which way the garden slopes, if at all. Paved areas will need to be built with a slight slope (see page 22) to remove surface water, and if the paving slabs have a cracked or uneven surface, the slope will need to be increased to prevent puddles from forming (see pages 24–5). This slope needs to be planned at the outset, as it will affect how much ground you need to excavate. If possible, plan the slope to be in the same direction as any existing slope on the ground, because this will reduce the amount of soil to be excavated and will also allow surface water to drain away more easily.

Ideally, patios should slope away from the house to ensure that any surface water is not trapped against the house wall. If this means that the patio would slope into higher ground, there are several options. A small area of paving 6–10 ft. wide could tip back to the house provided there are shrub beds against the wall into which any water could filter. Alternatively, introduce a slope running parallel to the house, which would take water into the beds to one side of the patio. If there are no beds, then lay a channel drain

against the house wall, which will direct water to a soakaway (see pages 22–3). Channels such as these may also be used if paving tips away from the house toward a retaining wall or bank. Paving and soil in beds adjacent to the house must be at least 6 in. below the insulation layer in the house wall to prevent wetness from creeping into the house. Paved areas that are at some distance from the house also need to be built on a slope, and in this case, the paving could be laid to tip toward the lawn or adjacent beds.

Measuring the surface slope

Setting out level pegs for paving requires a point of reference or a datum back to which all levels refer. Against the house, this could be the insulation layer. In the middle of the lawn, however, you will need to create a temporary reference point, or datum. To do this, knock a peg into the ground just to one side of your proposed area of paving, making sure that it is clearly visible at 6 in. above the existing ground level. Decide on the finished level of paving at one end of the patio (which may be the existing lawn level), then hold a level across the datum peg, measure down to your proposed finished level, and record the measurement. Remember

that your paving will have to have a slope across it, so calculate how much lower one end of the patio will be than the other (see page 22). Add this

Measuring the slope with a datum and level.

drop to the first measurement that you recorded, and this will represent the difference in height from the top of the reference point to the finished paving level at the lower end of the patio.

Maintaining the surface level

You can now excavate the area to the correct depth below the finished paving level and lay the underlying material (see pages 26–7) in position. When you are ready to start laying the paving, set up two string lines at right angles to each other, running along two sides of the proposed patio.

You can reuse the lines you used initially to mark out the shape of the patio. Pull them taut and fix at the correct level of the paving by passing them across the top of pegs that have

String lines used to indicate the finished level.

been driven in to mark the finished paving level. You may need to tap a nail into the peg to prevent the line from slipping off.

These lines can now be used to indicate the finished level, the slope, and the patio's edge. It will also help to set a temporary peg at the end of the patio, away from the string line, as this will give another level reference point to use when laying the slabs.

A temporary peg is a useful reference point.

Working with larger patios

On a large patio, you may need several pegs placed throughout the area in a grid pattern, which will help enormously when laying slabs. Once you have pegs set up at each corner at the right level, create a grid by running a string line across the tops of the pegs and knocking in additional pegs to the height of the line at intervals along its length. Pull lines from one side of the area to the other and repeat until the grid has been completed.

Creating a grid pattern.

Using a laser level

Setting in finished level pegs at some distance from each other using a level, straightedge, and tape measure is very impractical and laborious. Fortunately, there is a far quicker method—a laser level or other leveling equipment.

You can take a reading off the laser level when it is held on top of the first peg and then calculate what your next reading should be. The reading for the second peg will be the same as the previous one if the pegs are to be level, but must be calculated to include a slope as necessary. Place the staff on top of the second peg and continue

to knock the peg down until the laser records the correct level.

Reading a laser level.

Using the string method

There is an alternative to using a laser level that does not require such sophisticated equipment. Knock in two pegs level with each other, about 6 ft. apart, and then pull a string line across the top of the first peg, over the second, to a position at the other side of your proposed paving where you will need to fix a third peg. By gently lowering the line until it brushes the top of the second peg, you will create a level line that indicates the necessary height of your third peg.

Positioning the string line.

drainage

If water is not allowed to drain from paved surfaces, puddles will form, making the paving impractical because it will be slippery or icy. The water can also build up against walls and cause dampness. If your paving slopes toward a wall or bank, it is imperative to include in your plan a channel that will carry the water away from the garden and the house.

Calculating the slope

It is important that a paved area has a sufficient slope to remove water, but this should be subtle. There is no point in building a highly angled slope when something much more gentle would work perfectly well. The following figures can be used as a general guide:

Paving slabs (smooth and textured)
1:72 or 1 in. to 6 ft.

Riven slabs, natural stone, and bricks
1:60 or 1 in. to 5 ft.

Granite setts and other uneven surfaces
1:40 or 1 in. to 40 in.

Gravel surfaces
1:40 or 1 in. to 40 in.

For example, a natural stone patio that is to be 15 ft. wide would need a slope of 1:60 and a drop of 3 in. over its length. To create the required slope on an existing flat area, raise or excavate it by 3 in. Raising the level may not be possible if it is then too close to the insulating layer in the house wall, so the far end of the patio would have to be dug into the ground in order for the patio to slope away from the house. This obviously creates a level change and the need for drainage.

Gravel areas

Gravel areas also have to be laid to a slope, because although they are free-draining, water sits on the subbase.

Paved areas

A slope in only one direction may be used on narrow areas of paving up to 20 ft. wide. Wider areas may need a slope in two directions that meet at a central channel connecting to a drain. Other areas may need to be mounded, for example, a circular sitting area in a flat lawn. By lifting up the center point you create a slope, but the edge of the mound remains flush with the lawn.

Drainage channels and gullies

Open channels are available as custom-made units, or you can create a dish-shaped channel from bricks. Some channels have a removable steel grid that helps keep debris out of the drain. The channels carry water to a gully pot that can be fitted neatly into the paving. A pipe is connected to the outlet of this gully, which leads to the soakaway. These pipes should be laid to a gradient of 1:40 for pipes with a diameter of 4 in.

Soakaways

Soakaways are simply large holes dug into the ground and backfilled with large aggregate stones or gravel into which the surface water is piped. A geotextile membrane should be placed on top of the stones to separate them from the soil and turf

Soakaways

This cross section shows the installation of a drainage pipe to lead surface water into a soakaway set under an area of lawn from which it is separated by a geotextile membrane.

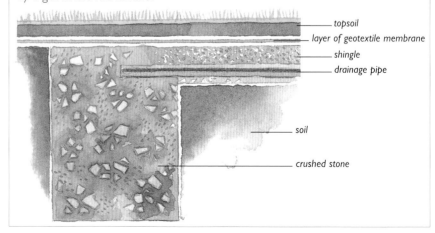

topsoil
layer of geotextile membrane
shingle
drainage pipe
soil
crushed stone

that can then be replaced over the top of the area. The soakaway needs to be of a minimum size of 40 × 40 × 40 in., and it should be dug about 10 ft. from the house. The base should be dug down at least 2 ft. into permeable ground. This can be tricky in heavy clay areas with a high water table, because the water will never drain away. In extreme cases, you can hire a contractor who will drill bore holes down to a permeable layer beneath the clay.

Piped French drain

As an alternative to a soakaway, you can create a French drain if you are laying an area of paving that has to tip toward a slope.

1 Excavate a trench along the length of the patio between the paving and the slope or wall. The trench only needs to be a spade's width and not too deep, although this depends on the overall slope. A geotextile membrane can be laid into the trench before laying down the pipe; this will extend the drain's life by preventing any soil from being washed into the pipe.

2 To ensure that the pipe drains correctly, you will need to apply a slope of about 1:60 along its length. Over a 10-ft. length, therefore, the pipe would need to fall by 2 in. from one end to the other. This means that the layer of gravel that the pipe will be laid on will need to be built up by about an extra 2 in. at one end to provide the slope. Spread the layer of gravel along the base of the trench, adding more to one end, and position the pipe.

3 You should then backfill over the top of the pipe with more gravel to about 2 in. from ground level. The pipe will be completely covered.

4 Once the trench has been completely backfilled with gravel, the geotextile membrane can be wrapped back over the top. Because the membrane is already inside the trench, the whole gravel and pipe system is protected within this membrane, which will help to prevent it from filling with silt. The membrane itself can be folded over and neatly tucked under the edge of the paving.

5 If the drain runs along the foot of a bank, topsoil and turf can be spread over the membrane up to paving level. Or, if the drain is against a wall, you can top the trench up with more gravel to the finished paving level.

steps AND RAMPS

The primary function of steps is to provide fast access from one level of the garden to another in much the same manner as stairs in a house. Outside in the garden, though, steps can be an attractive feature. They can be broader and deeper than internal steps, and they can meander and zigzag up slopes, offering interesting routes from bottom to top.

Designing steps

At a change of level, you might use steps instead of a low retaining wall, allowing one area to flow into another without interruption. The same steps can provide an added attraction if they are used as seating or surrounded with plantings. Low plants can be grown at the side of steps to tumble down and soften the construction, as well.

Ramps provide even gentler access than steps from one level to another and are useful for wheelchairs, wheelbarrows, and lawn mowers. They are not always attractive, and with a maximum gradient of 1:10 (see page 22), ramps can take up a lot of room in a small garden. Ramped steps require less space, as they combine ramps of 1:10 or 1:12 with low bump steps of about 4 in. at regular intervals.

Planning for steps

Steps need to be planned carefully. The height of risers and the depth of treads are important considerations, because otherwise the climb up the steps can be disconcerting and dangerous.

The maximum height for a riser should not be more than about 6 in., while the minimum height should not be less than 4 in. A comfortable tread depth is 15 in., though 18 in. is commonly used to fit the unit size of a paving slab. There is also a ratio of riser height to tread depth to consider, which means that the shallower the riser, the deeper the tread should be. Similarly, the steeper the riser, the narrower the tread should be. A good rule of thumb is: 2 × riser + tread = 26 in., although this can vary slightly.

Building steps

1 Before beginning construction, determine the height and depth of the steps needed. Measure the height of the bank by holding a straightedge out horizontally from the top of the bank, checking it with a level, and measuring down from the underside of the straightedge to the bottom of the bank. Determine the number of steps required by dividing the bank height by a sensible step height. To determine

Steps with brick risers

This shows steps that use brick risers built over the ends of the slab treads. A concrete foundation under the first riser gives strength to the structure.

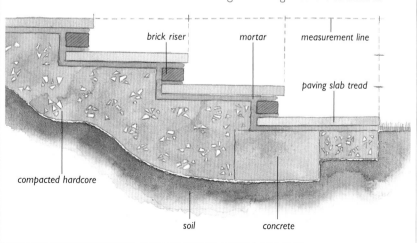

brick riser   mortar   measurement line

paving slab tread

compacted hardcore

soil   concrete

the depth of each tread, measure the length of the flight of steps along the straightedge, not down the slope, and divide this by the number of steps. If you need to change the dimensions of the steps, adjust them all by the same amount.

2 Clear the ground for the flight of steps and mark out their position. Excavate the bank, roughly cutting the steps into the ground.

3 Fix one peg at the bottom of the bank beyond the first tread and one at the top of the bank beyond the top riser. Tie a string line to these pegs, adjusting it down to indicate the final height of the treads. Check and adjust the shaping of the flight of steps against the string line, allowing for the riser and tread materials, and the mortar joints.

4 Dig a trench to make the foundation of the first step however wide you want your steps to be. Fill the trench with a firm concrete mix and level it off with the back of a shovel. Leave the concrete until it has completely hardened.

5 To make the first riser of the flight of steps, lay a row of bricks end to end into a firm mortar mix (see page 28) on top of the concrete foundation. Joint the brick units with mortar as you go. Lay a second row of bricks on top of the first row, if required, staggering the jointing pattern to make the step construction sturdy and secure.

6 Lay the foundation for the first tread by backfilling the first riser with a layer of compacted hardcore and level it off. Point the joints between the bricks in front of the riser, because these will be inaccessible once the tread has been placed into its position.

7 Cover the first tread with a thick layer of mortar. Position a slab on the tread so that it overhangs the riser by 2 in. This will cast a shadow line, masking the mortar joint. Lay the slab down, tapping it so that the top just touches the string line. Go on to finish the first tread and point the joints.

8 Build the next riser on top of the previous tread and continue to build the steps using the same method. Be sure that they all just touch the string, as shown. Check the depth of each tread and the height of each riser to ensure that you end up with the correct number of steps all built to the same dimensions.

base CONSTRUCTION

It is essential to lay paving on a firm base to get a professional finish. Otherwise, soils that may be prone to shrinking will transfer such movement straight through to the surface of the paving and crack the slabs. For this reason, topsoil and all loose ground must be removed first and replaced by an even layer of compacted hardcore or concrete.

Excavation

Once the area to be paved has been clearly marked out and level pegs have been set up, you can begin excavating for the base.

1 Unless you are intending to save the topsoil to be reused, dig straight down to the correct depth, allowing for the thickness of the paving and mortar bed plus approximately 3–4 in. for the depth of the subbase. Check the depth from time to time by measuring down with a steel tape measure from a level held across the datum peg. If level pegs have been set up around the area to indicate the finished patio height, pull a string line from one peg to another and measure down from the string line to check the depth of excavation.

2 Transfer the planned slope across the surface of the patio (see pages 22–3) to the subbase, making one side of the excavation deeper than the other. Begin by digging a trench along the back of the area, followed by one at the correct depth along the front, and then connect the two trenches at the right depth by excavating the area between them.

3 Excavate an area that is slightly wider than the proposed patio to ensure that the subbase extends underneath all the paving and to make laying the edge slabs easier. Dig out any soft spots and fill them with crushed stone.

4 Remove excavated material from the site with a wheelbarrow. Use a wheelbarrow with an air-filled tire to remove the material, and if you have to cross soft ground, set up a runway of scaffold planks to prevent the wheelbarrow from sinking into the ground. Make sure you do not overfill the wheelbarrow, because this will make it harder to push.

Materials

There are two layers of materials that form the base underneath paving. The first layer is the hardcore, or subbase, which is discussed here, and above this is the bedding material, or mortar, onto which the paving is laid (this is shown in detail on pages 28–9).

Crushed stone

The material that is commonly used for a subbase is crushed stone, which varies depending on the region where it was quarried. It is specified by its range of aggregate sizes: 1 ½ in. down to a fine dust, for example. This material is delivered loose or in 1-ton (20 cwt) bags.

It is best to avoid general builders' rubble for use under paving, as it tends to consist of broken slabs, bricks, and old lumps of mortar, none of which will compact down easily. The lack of fine material also prevents the hardcore from bonding into a cohesive layer, so settling may occur. This type of material is really only suitable to fill a deep excavation, which can then be capped over with a strong mix of reinforced concrete.

Lightweight concrete

An alternative to crushed stone is lightweight concrete, a weak concrete mix in the ratio of one part cement to ten or twelve parts all-in-ballast (mixed sizes of aggregate from a gravel pit), which can then be raked out and compacted in the same manner as crushed stone. Though this alternative is slightly more expensive, it is the best material to use over soft ground.

Stronger concrete mixes are only needed to form a layer over made-up ground, usually in a raised terrace. In this case, concrete in a mix of 1:6 should be poured through a grate of reinforcing steel that is supported so that the grate is sandwiched in the middle of a layer of concrete. The steel grate holds the concrete together in a raft to counter any settlement that would otherwise crack the paving.

Laying the subbase

1 When you are satisfied that you have excavated to the right depth, wheelbarrow in the crushed stone and roughly shovel it into position. Measure down from the string lines as before to check that the subbase is at the correct level. Remember that the material will compact down by about ten to fifteen percent and should therefore be left slightly raised to allow for this.

2 On large areas, lay timber rails at intervals across the base of the excavation in order to help you place the crushed stone at the correct depth. You should place the rails at the same depth as the finished layer of subbase and use them as a guide up to which you can rake the stone. Then remove the rails and backfill their place with stone.

3 Use a plate compactor on the whole area to compact the material, using a handheld tamper to deal with any awkward corners. After you have finished the compaction, check the depth again, spreading and compacting hardcore over any low spots. The area will then be ready for bedding down the paving.

Concrete being poured through a steel grate.

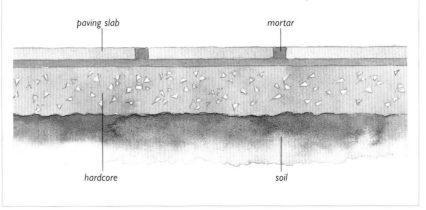

A typical paving construction
This shows the different layers needed to construct a paved patio or path. The slabs are laid on a full bed of mortar over a subbase of compacted hardcore.

paving slab   *mortar*

hardcore   *soil*

bedding, pointing, AND PLANTING

Paving slabs are laid on mortar, a mix of sand and cement. Mortar is also used for filling or pointing the joints between the slabs in some types of paving. Plants can be used to soften the edges of the new paving, while some can even be planted within the paved area to release their fragrance when touched.

Bedding material

Mortar is the bedding material that is spread over the subbase (see pages 26–7) and onto which the paving units are laid. Mortar for paving is a mix of sharp sand (not soft builder's sand), cement, and water. Depending on the amount of material you need, you can either have the sand delivered loose, in 1-ton (20 cwt) sacks, or in 55-lb. bags for small jobs.

The mix of sharp sand and cement sets as hard as concrete and forms an excellent bedding course for paving. Sand on its own is not really good enough as a bedding material for paving, because ground water or any water that filters down between the slabs will start to erode the sand and cause the slabs to settle. The only time

sand should be used as bedding is for interlocking brick paving units. Then using a board, a layer of sand can be dragged out level (screeded) over the subbase onto which bricks are placed and then vibrated down into the sand with a plate compactor. With this method of paving, the interlocking bricks act as a flexible surface. This paving is ideal for making driveways, because it spreads the heavy load of a vehicle throughout the area. To be successful, however, it is essential to use a dry sand bed. The introduction of cement would create a rigid construction that doesn't have the same load-spreading qualities.

Mortar mixes

Mortar mixes are indicated in the ratio of cement to sand, with the most

common mixes ranging from 1:3 to 1:12. A mix somewhere in the middle, about 1:6, is suitable for most types of paving. However, a much weaker mix of 1:10 is acceptable for stone paving, because the flagstones are so heavy they are almost self supporting. In this case, there is no real need to use a very strong mix—it would just be a waste of cement and money.

The amount of water in a mix is a matter of judgment—if the mortar is too wet, it may not actually support the paving units. Wet mortar is also messy to work with and can splash and stain the paving. The mortar needs to be just firm enough to support the paving units while they are tapped down to the correct level.

Fairly dry mortar mixes can be used for bedding small paving units such as bricks: screed out an area of mortar, place the bricks on top, and tamp them down into position. In this instance, the dry mix can be a fairly strong 1:4 mortar in order to hold these smaller paving units firmly in place. The edges of patios or pathways can also be held firm using a technique known as "haunching." Here, mortar or concrete may be spread out and smoothed along the outside edge of the patio, stopping just below the surface of the paving in order to prevent any side-to-side movement.

Compacting paving bricks into sand.   A mix of cement and sand makes up mortar.

Mixing mortar by hand

For bedding mortar, use a shovel to measure out the sand and cement. For pointing mortar, it is essential that each mix is consistent in terms of strength of color when dry. Therefore, it is better to use a dry bucket rather than a shovel as an accurate gauge of material quantities.

1 Shovel the correct amount of sand into a pile on a dry board and tip the cement onto it. Use a shovel to mix them until an even color is achieved.

2 Make a crater in the middle of the pile and add water. Turn the dry mix into it, trying not to let any water escape.

3 You should continue to work the first lot of water in, but if it seems that the mix is still too dry, form a crater again and add a little more water. Keep turning in the material until the mix is moist, not wet, and can be easily worked with a shovel. Be careful not to add too much water at once, as the mix may become too sloppy.

4 Next, slide a shovel underneath the mortar and turn it upside down. Continue to do this a few times before spreading it out on a board. Then move the shovel back and forth through the mix using a chopping action. This ensures that the mortar is blended to an even consistency.

Using a mixer

If you have a large amount of mortar to mix, use a mixer. An electric mixer is easier and quieter to use than a gas-powered machine. Set up the mixer close to your sand and cement supplies,

A mixer is useful for making a lot of mortar.

but face it away from the paving area to avoid splashes. If you have to do the mixing on an existing driveway or paved surface, make sure your wheelbarrow is standing on a large board over a sheet of plastic to prevent mortar from splashing and staining the surface. Ideally, mix mortar on an area of soil, lawn, or old concrete.

You should limit the amount of mortar you make to that which can be used in an hour or two, otherwise it will be wasted. Once you have placed your mixture in the machine, you will need to add water while it is running to achieve the correct consistency. The mortar should not be runny, but it should still fall off the blades.

Once your mix is ready, you can tip it into a wheelbarrow and get to work. At the end of the day, turn off the mixer and scrape out any excess mortar. Add water and a couple of broken bricks to help break the remaining mortar loose.

Laying paving

There are two methods for laying paving stones with mortar: Either apply five spots to the ground beneath each slab and tap them into position, or lay a full bed of mortar and place slabs on top. The joints for both methods should be about ³⁄₈ in. wide.

The five spot method

This method supports the slab on all corners as well as in the middle, and it makes it easy to tap the slab down into position. However, it does create more of a problem when pointing up later, because the pointing mix may disappear to fill in the void under the slab when pushed into the joints. There is also the possibility that water will sit under the slabs, resulting in the potential problem of slabs moving due to freezeing and thawing.

The mortar bed method

A full bed of mortar is the strongest method, because the whole slab is supported and water is kept out. Spread a layer of mortar over the hardcore base. Use a trowel to create ridges and furrows in the mortar so that when the slab is tapped down, the

The five spot method.

mortar has a space in which to move and you end up with a solid bed about 1½ in. deep.

The mortar bed method.

Pointing techniques

Pointing is the process of filling the joints between the paving slabs with mortar in order to keep water from seeping down between the slabs. Pointing also prevents weeds from growing up through the gaps.

Pointing up open joints

1 Mortar for pointing up paving needs to be much stronger than bedding mortar, because it is subject to weathering. If it is too weak, it may crumble due to frost action.

The most common mix is 1:4 (one part cement to two parts sharp sand and two parts soft sand). Soft sand is introduced so that you can rub the joint smooth. You may prefer a slightly weaker mix of 1:5 or 1:6, because this encourages attractive mosses to become established.

The pointing mix needs to be crumbly, so make sure that it is not too wet. You should never do any of your pointing when it is raining or if the paving is wet, because the mix may stain the paving.

2 Use a brick to push the mix into the joints between the slabs, making sure they are completely filled.

3 Once all the joints are full, use a piece of pipe to rub the mortar smooth to form neat channels. These channels allow any surface water to run off easily. The channels will be less pronounced if a weak mortar mix is used in the joints, because mosses will soften their appearance.

4 After you have left the mortar to dry for a few hours, any excess mortar that is on the surface can then be scraped off the surface of the slabs. Use a soft brush to sweep the paving clean. This ensures that

no remaining mortar, which would stain the surface of the patio, will be ground in.

Butt-jointed paving

There are some types of paving slabs and bricks that can be laid butt jointed, which means that they are laid tightly against each other without a mortar joint. Take care when using this method, because it only takes a few grains of dry bedding mortar trapped between the paving to open up the

Laying butt-jointed paving.

joint, which will cause the jointing pattern to be ruined. After laying butt-jointed bricks, brush some fine, dry sand over the surface of the paving to help form a tight seal between the

Brushing sand in to seal the butt joints.

bricks. You will not be able to use this method for stone paving and some concrete paving slabs with irregular edges, because they cannot easily be laid together tightly.

Planting

There are many plants that blend in well with paving in different areas of the garden, and some of these plants can even withstand being walked on occasionally. You can plant up areas around the edges or inside the paving. For example, helianthemum, aubrieta, and cerastium will thrive in dry, sunny terraces, where they form mats to creep over and soften the edges of

Plants can be placed among paving.

paving. These plants all enjoy the dry, free-draining environment provided by gravel surfaces or the gritty compost that can be used to fill joints between paving. Plants such as these work well in stepping-stone paths, patios, and gravel walkways.

Where the joints between slabs are too narrow to introduce small plants, you can sow the seeds of herbs or alpines that will quickly establish to soften the paving. Varieties of creeping thyme and mat-forming chamomile, *Chamaemelum nobile* 'Treneague,' can be walked on to release their wonderful fragrance. Other plants, such as blue fescue (*Festuca glauca*), as well as many varieties of fern that are not mat-forming, simply look great growing through a graveled surface.

Plants also associate well with pathways in wooded areas, softening the edges of bark paths or growing up between slabs in stepping-stone paths. Bugleweed, dead nettle, and gaultheria all do well in these positions. Ivy, periwinkle, and Irish moss will also be successful, but they will need to be controlled as they are invasive.

Ground cover for sunny sites
Armeria (thrift)
Aubrieta (rockcress)
Chamaemelum nobile 'Treneague'
(Roman chamomile)
Helianthemum (rock rose)
Saxifraga (saxifrage)
Thymus (thyme)
Ground cover for shady sites
Ajuga (bugleweed)
Hedera (ivy)
Lamium (dead nettle)
Lysimachia nummularia (creeping Charlie)
Soleirolia (Irish moss)
Vinca (periwinkle)

good working PRACTICE

The logistics of building a small project in your own garden need to be thought through very carefully. You will want to make sure that everything is done properly, and you should be especially vigilant with regard to safety issues. Follow the simple suggestions below to create a safe, well-run construction site while building your new garden surfaces.

Safety and protection

If you are not used to physical work, do not try to do too much in a hurry. Warm up and stretch as you would for any other physical activity. Remember to lift properly, with your knees bent and your back kept straight, and always ask for help when lifting heavy equipment or materials.

If you have long hair, tie it back out of the way, especially when using machinery. Wear suitable clothes that neither restrict movement nor flap around. Rain gear is essential for rainy days, because there is no point in working while you are cold and wet. Always wear steel-toed boots for construction work and a pair of strong gloves when handling sharp-edged concrete slabs or cement.

When using a slab cutter or a hammer and bolster, you must wear goggles to protect your eyes. A protective mask will keep out the dust, and ear protection would also be a wise precaution.

If you use high-voltage electrical equipment on-site, then you must make sure that circuit breakers are installed to cut off the power in case the cable becomes damaged. Suppliers can provide transformers, which are the safest option.

Allowing plenty of time to carry out tasks means that you can take proper care, whereas if you try to rush through a job, it may cause you to leave potentially dangerous tools and materials scattered around that will cause other people harm.

Power tools, saws, and other potentially hazardous equipment obviously need to be kept out of the reach of children and should always be locked away at the end of the day. Children like climbing over things, so always make sure that your materials are stacked and stored properly.

It is also difficult to be responsible for children when you are using noisy machinery, so make sure that they are being supervised well out of the way before you start any work, and be sure to remove the ignition key when machines are not in use so that accidents cannot happen.

Excavations need to be covered over with strong boards, and ideally the site should be cordoned off from the rest of the garden (see opposite).

The correct way to lift heavy materials.

Using a slab cutter.

Using a hammer and bolster.

Storing materials

If possible, try to unload materials next to where they will be used to avoid handling them more than once. This is rarely possible, and you may find you have to unload the materials onto the driveway first. Store loose materials such as sand and gravel on plywood boards away from each other—if they get mixed up, you will find it frustrating to try to lay slabs on mortar that contains the occasional piece of gravel.

Sand and gravel can be hauled in by the truckload or delivered in large, heavy-duty bags, which hold about 1 ton. Bagged sand and gravel are slightly more expensive, but they are much more convenient, because the bags keep the material clean and take up less space. Cement is delivered in 50-lb. bags; you should stack the bags on pallets or boards and cover them with plastic sheets, ideally in a shed so that they do not get damp. Arrange paving slabs on their edges, side by side, and stack bricks in piles. Keep sand and cement off driveways, as they will stain the surface, and move pallets of slabs off the driveway as quickly as possible, as the weight can dent some surfaces.

Paving slabs should be stored on their edges.

Stack bricks neatly on top of each other.

Construction day

Keep an eye on the weather forecast when you are planning your days for construction. Although some jobs can be done in the rain, it is not much fun, and you can end up making far more mess than is really necessary. Consider your neighbors, too. You might want to get an early start on a Sunday morning, but they may not appreciate having their one morning to sleep in interrupted by a noisy cement mixer. An electric mixer is quieter than a gas-powered mixer, but it is still wise to plan all your noisier jobs for a more suitable time of day. Dust is a problem that cannot always be avoided, so check to see if your neighbors' windows are open before using a slab cutter, and consider using attachments that keep the disk dampened down to reduce dust.

Try to work logically and in sensible stages, giving yourself time for breaks in order to stand back, assess progress, and plan the next task. Think each part of the job through before beginning, especially when you are cutting slabs or other materials. And always double-check measurements before making the final cut to avoid mistakes and expensive waste.

Completing the day's work

Leave plenty of time at the end of the day to clean the cement mixer and hand tools, particularly those that have been used for mortar and concrete, as the materials will set hard and ruin the tools if you do not clean them off. Then make sure that you immobilize the machines and cover all the materials safely.

Paved areas are best left covered with plastic sheets that are held down by boards, especially if there is any chance of rain or frost.

Ensure that the site is left completely safe by covering any trenches and excavated areas for paving with sturdy boards. Ideally, you should cordon off the whole area with brightly colored tape or temporary plastic fencing. Lights may be unnecessary in your backyard, but they are an absolute must for leading visitors safely past construction work in the front of your house. Battery-powered safety lamps, along with rolls of plastic fencing, tape, and warning cones, may all be obtained from most home-supply stores.

Plastic fencing cordons off construction areas.

tools AND EQUIPMENT

It is important to invest in good-quality tools that will last you a lifetime. The tools needed for garden construction have been placed in three categories here: tools for groundwork, paving, and woodwork, while the section on rental tools covers machinery you may prefer not to buy. Each photograph illustrates the tool that is described directly above it.

Groundwork tools

Beetle Similar to a sledgehammer, but with a round, flat head; ideal for knocking in wooden posts.

Crowbar A long, heavy iron bar for levering out old concrete or rocks.
Pitchfork It is extremely useful to have a heavy pitchfork when you are digging up ground.
Mattock This is similar in appearance to a pickax, though the head has one flat blade that makes it ideal for hooking out shallow trenches. It also has one blade, which is similar to an ax head and is useful for chopping through old roots.
Measuring tape, 100 ft. This tape is essential for surveying and setting up. It is particularly useful to have two such tapes for triangulation.
Measuring wheel This is a useful tool if you need to measure a large garden.

In such a case, it is much more practical than measuring tapes.

Pickax This is useful for breaking up hard ground or old concrete.

Shovel This is a multipurpose tool for digging out soil as well as for spreading hardcore, sand, and mortar.
Sledgehammer This tool can be described as a long-handled, heavy

hammer, and it is used for breaking up old paved surfaces.

Spade A heavy-duty spade should be used for digging up ground.
Timber pegs These are short, pointed pegs that are needed for most jobs.
Wheelbarrow You should aim to buy a heavy-duty barrow with an air-filled tire suitable for carrying heavy loads over uneven ground.

Paving tools

Bolster This is a broad, flat-headed chisel used for cutting bricks.

Broom A stiff broom is useful for cleaning off dirty paving, while a soft brush is essential for sweeping paving after pointing or brushing sand into paving bricks.

Bucket This is a heavy-duty pail that can be used for water, but also for measuring sand and cement in a pointing mix.

Club hammer This is a short-handled, heavy hammer, which is often known as a "lump hammer." It is used with a bolster for cutting bricks and with a cold chisel for breaking old concrete. Its handle can also be used for tapping down paving bricks.

Cold chisel Used alongside a club hammer to break up old concrete.

Float This is a small, flat metal tool that is used for smoothing out concrete.

Goggles, gloves, and ear protectors These should all be worn when cutting paving and when using concrete breakers.

Hacksaw This small saw is used for cutting metal edging.

Line and pins This refers to short metal pins that can be pushed into soil or mortar and between which a string line is pulled taut to indicate the edge and finished height of paving.

Measuring tape, 10 ft. This is a retractable tape that is essential for the detailed measuring of paving and woodwork.

Plastic sheets Purchase a few large sheets of plastic, because they can be used to cover paving once it has been

pointed in order to keep the rain off.

Pointing trowel This is a small, triangular-shaped trowel that looks like a brick trowel but is used for filling in the mortar joints in paving.

Tamper This tool is used for compacting small areas of hardcore.

Rubber maul A rubber mallet for tapping down flagstones or railroad ties.

Set square A wooden triangle that can be used for setting out paving.

Spirit level A 3-ft. long level is ideal, especially one with a bubble on the top edge, for laying paving.

Straightedge A planed length of wood essential for setting pegs level and paving to the correct slope.

Watering can A heavy-duty can is useful for adding water to mortar.

Woodwork tools

Adjustable spanner This is used for tightening nuts and bolts for deck posts and beams.

Claw hammer Used for banging in nails and also for pulling out old nails.

Cordless drill This is a lightweight drill powered by a rechargeable battery, which is far more convenient than using an electric drill with a cord. It can be fitted with screwdriver attachments for the different types of screws, which makes easy work of fixing and undoing screws.

Paintbrushes Always choose good-quality brushes for applying stain to wooden decks.

Panel saw This is a general-purpose saw for most of your woodworking needs. A smaller tenon saw can also be used for detailed joint work.

Plane This tool is used for smoothing down wood to produce a neat, planed finish.

Surform A similar action to using a plane is required with this tool, which takes rough edges off sawed timber.

Try square This is a set square that is used for woodworking.

Wood chisel This is used for cutting out joints in wooden posts when creating decking joists.

Wooden mallet Used with a wood chisel. You can hit the chisel with a mallet to create a greater force.

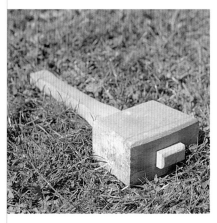

Using these tool lists
To keep long, repetitive lists of tools from appearing at the end of each project, only the necessary categories of equipment (groundwork and paving, for example) have been recorded. If one item from another section is also required to complete the project, it is listed individually.
Any necessary rental equipment is also shown at the end of the list. Therefore, you will need to refer back to this section as you are planning the projects that you wish to carry out in your own garden.

Rental tools

Chain saw Logs and railroad ties can be cut easily with a chain saw. There are, however, strict guidelines concerning the rental of chain saws. A company should only rent a chain saw out to a member of the public if they are convinced that it is the correct tool for the job and the customer demonstrates the ability to use it properly. The rental store can actually refuse to rent out a saw if they have any doubts about the customer. They will give out protective equipment with the saw, and this must be worn at all times when using the chain saw. Make sure that you also follow all the instructions they give you, as they are important for your safety.

Circular saw If you have many beams and deck boards to cut, then a circular saw is the best tool to use.

Concrete breaker An electric breaker is essential for breaking up areas of old concrete.

Concrete mixer It is far easier to mix concrete with a machine than by hand. Small mixers that fit onto a stand are the simplest to manage and transport. Both gas and electric mixers are available—the electric type is much quieter and therefore more neighbor-friendly.

Laser level This is an excellent piece of surveying equipment that can be operated by just one person. It can be rented very cheaply by the day.

Plate compactor This is the mechanical version of the handheld tamper, and it is mainly used for compacting large areas of hardcore. However, it can also be used as a tool for bedding down paving bricks once they have been laid.

Skip loader This is like a little dump truck; it can be loaded with soil and driven to the side of a skip. Then the load is raised up and tipped out.

Slab cutter This gas-powered machine is used to cut paving slabs. An attachment allows a hose to be fixed to it that dribbles water along the cut when in use to keep dust down.

Tracked excavator A whole range of excavating machinery can be rented, which will save you an awful lot of hand digging. Tracked vehicles are useful on uneven ground, but rubber tracks are essential if you have to drive over any tarmac roads.

Vibrating rollers These provide great compaction, but they are unwieldy.

paths

planning for paths

In addition to the important practical function of linking areas of the garden, carefully designed pathways make dramatic features. A straight path provides a strong visual link between one end of the garden and another, drawing the eye along its length with definite purpose. On the other hand, curving, meandering paths lead intriguingly into the distance, encouraging people to walk along them to discover what lies at the end.

Function and style Pathways usually have the practical function of providing access from one part of the garden to another. They are also essential for maintenance; for example, they could provide access along the back of a shrub border to trim a hedge. Often, paths are multifunctional—one laid around the edge of a lawn provides access to adjacent planting and also negates the need for laborious edging. The same path may serve as a circular bicycle track for children. The style of path can be chosen to match the overall style and mood of the garden, and this can be achieved by using the same material as the patio so that they echo one another. As paths lead away from the house, the materials can be spaced with gaps for plants to fill, creating a much softer appearance. As the atmosphere of the garden changes into a more relaxed style with drifts of naturalizing bulbs, a grass path may be introduced or a path of wood chips laid through more wooded areas.

Design choices Straight paths give direct access from one point to another, although introducing a simple turn in the path around a clump of shrubs will add more interest without greatly increasing the distance. A zigzag path will make a long, narrow garden seem wider, unlike a straight path, which will appear to shorten the view to the end. A circular path will have a similar effect, allowing you to stroll around the garden rather than just take a quick walk to the end and back. The surface pattern of a path is another design factor to consider. Brick paths laid to a running bond along the length of the path accentuate the direction and stimulate quicker movement, while the same pattern laid across the path appears to broaden the width and encourages a more leisurely walk. This same effect can be created with rectangular paving slabs, and even with a

Metal grid over water.

Concrete slabs in ground cover.

Cobbles and setts.

Loose aggregate.

The style of pathway is key when designing your garden layout: the crisp, clean lines of the smooth, pale slabs across water (top left) would complement an urban or minimalist garden. The meandering timber pathway surrounded by natural planting (top right) would be more suited to an informal country garden. The straight brick path (above) draws the eye to the end but the repeat of the pattern and the elegant borders encourage the walker to linger awhile.

Bricks laid across the width of a path can make a pathway look wider and encourage people to take their time as they amble along it.

wooden boardwalk. Surfaces such as natural stone setts or cobblestones, which are not completely smooth underfoot, will tend to slow movement down, as will surfaces where ground-cover plants have been allowed to grow in the joints or soften the edges. Stepping-stones can be used for visual effect, but must be laid close together if they are to be walked on. Mosaics of pebbles and ceramics laid in the surface of a path will create interest and so naturally slow you down. Other types of paving with a textured surface may be laid through shaded areas or on slight inclines where extra grip is needed. The width of a path will vary to suit its use. A broad path is often used where a slower pace is anticipated, and 4 ft. is needed for two people to stroll comfortably side by side. Narrower paths are fine for quick access, while a single line of bricks may be laid to create a visual, rather than practical, link.

Types of pathways Most garden materials can be used to form the surface of a path, and even grass or plants such as bugleweed (*Ajuga*) and dead nettle (*Lamium*)

Stepping-stones can be used for visual effect, but they must be laid close together if they are to be walked on.

can be grown to form a walkway for occasional use. Wood chips work well in a wooded setting, especially if laid over a base of hardcore to keep the path from becoming too wet and muddy. Most loose aggregates can be laid as a path, including gravel, broken tiles, pebbles, and even aluminum and copper granules, though they need to be retained with an edging. Self-setting gravel is a useful material for less-ornamental areas of the garden. This material is raked out and compacted with a wet roller to create a firm path with a natural appearance. Solid surfaces make the most durable paths, although some still need an edge restraint. Many types of paving bricks and concrete setts are compacted into a sand bed and locked together to create a firm surface, but it is the edging that keeps any joints from opening up and the path from deteriorating. Other paving units, such as natural stone flags or concrete paving slabs, are bedded on mortar to form a rigid surface, either as a solid path or laid through a flexible surface to create a strong directional line. Railroad ties or log rounds can also be laid for the same effect. Small paving units, such as brick or broken stone pavings, are ideal for curved paths.

The following projects illustrate the range of pathways that can be incorporated to suit the different areas of the garden—none of them require help from contractors.

Wood is an extremely versatile material to consider when planning and building a pathway. Jagged lengths of wood joined together in an uneven way (above left) provide an original and rustic walkway across a stream. On the other hand, stone slabs surrounded by a bed of gravel (above right) can provide a tantalizing walkway to connect two areas of a garden.

Natural slate.

Bricks in a basket-weave pattern.

Bricks in a running-bond pattern.

Log rounds with loose gravel.

stepping-STONES

Stepping-stones are ideal for making a path that is used only occasionally. They can be discreet, harmonizing with the garden's natural lines, or they can provide a strong visual sense of direction by leading the eye to a particular part of the garden.

1 Before cutting any turf, plan your desired pattern, laying the slabs out on the surface. Plan the spacing for the stride of the person who will use the path most often, with gaps that allow for a gentle stroll. If laying a path through ground cover, space stones carefully to minimize damage to plants, as most will withstand only the occasional footfall. Of course, if stepping-stones are being laid purely for their visual impact, then the spacing is not as critical.

2 Once all the slabs are in position, mark them out using a spade to notch around the edges, then set the slabs to one side. Dig out the turf and soil to an area slightly larger than the slab itself to give room for your fingers when you place the stones in position. Stepping-stones through a firm lawn area require very little base construction, so you will only need to dig out about 2 in. to allow for the thickness of the slab, plus a shallow depth of bedding sand.

MATERIALS

Sharp sand

Hardcore

Mortar

Paving slabs: 18 x 18 in.
12 x 12 in.

Fine soil

Grass seed

TOOLS

Groundwork tools

Paving tools

1 Lay the slabs out in the desired pattern to get the spacing right before you start to cut the turf.

2 Use a spade to mark an area slightly bigger than the edges of the slabs to give room for your fingers.

KNOW YOUR MATERIALS

Paving slabs can be laid in diamonds, squares, or even in random sizes, and they do not need to be laid as single slabs either—broad bands of paving with grass or ground-cover joints look equally effective in the garden. When paving slabs are made, pigments and aggregates can be added to the concrete mix in order to produce a range of muted colors. Different molds can also create a variety of surface finishes. You should therefore feel free to experiment with the numerous combinations of color and texture that are available commercially. Try mixing various different colored slabs together.

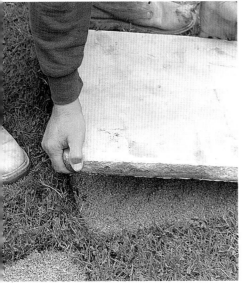

3 Gently lay the slab into position on a thin bed of sharp sand. A bed of mortar is not usually necessary when laying stepping-stones.

3 | Next spread a thin layer of sharp sand across the bottom of the first slab bed. Since the slabs for a stepping-stone path are isolated from one another, it does not matter if they move a bit after they are laid, so there is usually no need for a mortar bed. However, if the ground is loose, wet, or mounded, you could replace the sand with hardcore and a weak mix of sand and cement. Simply dig down an additional 3 in. to accommodate the base.

Move one of the slabs into position, then tap it down with a maul or club hammer on a block of wood until it lies flush with the lawn. It is essential that no slabs finish higher than the lawn surface, as this will form a dangerous edge that one may trip on and can create problems when mowing. Slabs should also flow with any slight slopes on the existing lawn, but there is no need to use a level. Once all the slabs have been laid, you may need to fill around the edges with fine soil and grass seed.

wood chip and
LOG ROUNDS PATH

Chips of bark and wood offer a soft, fragrant surface underfoot, reminiscent of woodland walks, and they are ideal for creating curved or winding pathways.

MATERIALS

Treated wood-path edging
4 x 1 in.

Pointed pegs 2 x 2 x 18 in.

Galvanized nails

Sharp sand

Hardcore

Log rounds

Path-grade bark or wood chips

TOOLS

Groundwork tools

Woodwork tools

Maul

Club hammer

Wood straightedge:
2 x 3 x 72 in.

Plate compactor

Chain saw

1 | Mark out the position of the path according to your plan. The specifics of lines and curves are not as critical with wood chip paths as they are with those built from slabs or bricks, where joint sizes can be affected. Clear the ground of vegetation, and remove loose soil down to a depth of about 4 in. If the surrounding area is full of weeds, lay plastic sheeting, which will help keep them from growing up through the surface and also keep the hardcore from pushing down into the wet soil.

To make the edging, drive in wood pegs along the path edges. Then position the treated wood path edgings and nail them back to the pegs at 40-in. intervals. Then spread hardcore to a depth of 3–4 in., rake it out, and compact it down.

2 | Next, place the log rounds out on the pathway in their approximate positions, and then move them to fit your

1 When you have laid the edging, scatter hardcore over the whole path surface to a depth of about 4 in.

2 Lay the log rounds in approximate positions to fit the step length of the person who will use the path most often.

KNOW YOUR MATERIALS

Log rounds: These are slices of old tree trunks that can be cut from any type of wood, but hardwood rounds like oak, beech, and ash will last longer than those cut from conifer trunks. Log rounds need not be too thick, between 3–4 in. is ideal; any bigger, and they would be too heavy, and the job would require additional excavation.

Wood chips: Come in many chip grades, with some sold specifically as path grade. Bagged material can readily be bought from garden centers and large home improvement stores, or delivered direct in 1-ton bags. If you are covering a very large area, it is possible to obtain bulk truckloads direct from the supplier.

exact step length or the step length of the person who will use the path most often. Along a tree-lined walk, position them for a gentle stroll. If the log rounds are purely for ornamental effect, their positioning is less important. However, you will find it is more visually appealing if they are staggered, rather than laid in a straight line.

3 Once you are satisfied with the line of log rounds, mark around each one with a spade or shovel, then put the rounds aside and dig out the hardcore from beneath them. The aim should be for the log round to finish flush with the edging boards at the sides of the path. Dig out to the depth of the log round plus an allowance for sand. Any hardcore that is dug out should be spread over the path, while any excavated soil must be spread to one side to prevent any soft spots from forming. Continue digging out the positions for all the log rounds.

4 Next sprinkle a thin layer of sharp sand under each round to help bed it down and to keep the base relatively dry.

There is no need for any hardcore under the rounds, because they are sturdy enough without it and it does not matter if they move a little. Work each log round down into position by hand.

5 Lay a straightedge across each log round so that it stretches from one side of the path to the other. If the straightedge rests on top of the log round and on each edging board, then the round is level and you can move on to the next one. Otherwise, tap down the round with a maul until the straightedge sits flush across the path. Continue to lay and tap down all the log rounds in this manner.

6 Now turn the straightedge along the length of the path, laying the wood across three or four of the rounds. Tap the rounds down with the maul until they all sit flush with the underside of the wood. This will ensure they do not create an uneven hazard along the length of the path that could cause someone to trip and fall.

3 Once you have decided on the positioning of the rounds, put them to one side and dig out the hardcore and soil from beneath them.

4 Sprinkle a thin layer of sharp sand underneath each round, and then work them down into position by hand.

5 Lay a straightedge across the path to check that the rounds are level with the edging.

Fill the foundation next to each log round by ramming the hardcore in with a club hammer.

7 Finally, using a shovel, spread bark or wood chips over the surface around the log rounds to a depth of about 1 in. You may find it easier to apply the final touches by hand, pushing the bark neatly around each log round.

Alternative materials

Bark and wood chips form a soft, dry, nonslip path surface that is especially appropriate for children—wood chips make a soft landing during rough and tumble playing. However, if you are looking for a firmer surface in a more formal part of the garden, gravel makes a fine alternative to bark chips. Additionally, gravel provides a nice contrast in color and texture to the log rounds.

The preparation of the hardcore base is exactly the same as for a surface of wood chips, leaving a depth of approximately 1 in. to be filled with gravel. Gravel and crushed slate, which is darker, both look good in a fairly natural setting. Shovel the gravel into place, and work the stone down around each log round by hand to produce a neat finish. Use a soft brush to clear any loose stones from the tops of the rounds.

Alternative methods

If you are already using wood chips as a mulch (loose material used to insulate the soil) for the shrubby undergrowth of a woodland-style garden, you could simply extend the area of chips away from the plants to provide a surface to walk upon, which also forms a link between the plants and path. This type of path is fine for occasional use, but it will not stand up to heavy wear and soon deteriorates if the ground is boggy.

For a less formal and adventurous walk in the garden, particularly appropriate for children, simply lay log rounds on their own as stepping-stones in a tree-lined area of your yard or through an area of the garden that is often bogged down.

6 Lay a wooden straightedge along the path to make sure that all the rounds are even and to avoid the possibility of anyone tripping.

7 Spread a layer of bark or wood chips over the path to a depth of approximately 1 in.

Alternative materials: Laying down gravel will provide a firmer surface and will offer a contrast in color and texture.

railroad tie and
GRAVEL PATH

With bushy pockets of semiwild plants appearing to reclaim the pathway, this type of railroad tie path conjures up both the reassuring solidity and the romance of bygone railways.

1 | Mark out the pathway and excavate to the full depth of a railroad tie over the whole pathway, allowing for 5 in. of hardcore and 1 in. of gravel. Wheel in the hardcore and spread it over the whole area. (Some hardcore will be removed to accommodate the railroad ties, but it is easier at this stage simply to cover the entire path base.) Compact down the layer of hardcore, leaving a gap approximately 1 in. below the finished path level to allow for the depth of gravel. Next, measure out the length of edging required for the path, and cut the metal edging material to size with a hacksaw. Some form of edging is essential to prevent the erosion that will inevitably be caused by people walking close to the sides.

2 | Position the edging strips along both sides of the path and bang them down to the finished height of the path using a club hammer. The strips can either be laid in the gaps

MATERIALS

Railroad ties

Hardcore

Metal edging

Battens

Sharp sand

Gravel

Ground-cover plants

Beach pebbles

TOOLS

Groundwork tools

Hacksaw

Club hammer

Chain saw

Maul

Household tamper

Straightedge

1 Once you have excavated the pathway area, you can begin edging your path. Here we are using metal to give a crisp, clean finish.

2 If you choose to, you can place the edging all the way along your path, and then bang it down to the correct height.

KNOW YOUR MATERIALS

Railroad ties: Available as either treated softwood or as hardwood. Softwood ties gain their durability by being heavily impregnated with tar, which also makes them rather dirty to handle. In shady conditions, this may not be a problem, but if you are laying the path in a sunny location, the tar may be drawn out of the wood in very hot weather. For this reason, hardwood may be the better choice.

Edging: Metal edging made for this purpose is readily available in lengths of 40 in. They usually have a thickness of $\frac{1}{8}$ in., which makes them very easy to cut with a hacksaw, as well as to bend to form a curve.

between the railroad ties, or as we have done here, in a continuous strip outside the ends of the ties, which avoids laborious cutting.

3 Next measure out and mark the correct length of railroad tie for the particular design of your path. Because ties are normally 8 ft. long, you might want to plan your design around 4-ft. lengths, which will help to avoid waste and still give a good width of wood to walk on. You should also consider whether you want to stagger the length of the cross ties in the pattern, in which case you will need to measure out different lengths of ties and cut the edging strips accordingly. The pattern of different-length railroad ties can be quite random, perhaps one long one followed by two short ones and then another long one. Staggering the ties introduces a sense of movement and creates a space at one end of the tie where you can plant ground cover. It also keeps the path from looking too much like a railroad track!

4 Now cut the tie lengths according to your chosen measurements. You will first need to lay the tie on battens to keep it off the ground—it will take two people to lift a full-size tie into position. If there are only one or two railroad ties to cut, you should be able manage with a bow saw. However, you might want to use a chain saw to make easy work of any cutting, especially if the path is long. Chain saws are available for personal rental, along with all the protective clothing (see page 37), but if you do not feel confident, you can always employ a contractor to carry out this part of the job.

5 Carry the cut ties to the path and lay them on the hardcore in their correct positions. When you are happy with the layout, mark around each one with a spade and set them to one side. Excavate a trench through the hardcore for each one, allowing for both the depth of the ties and a thin bed of sharp sand. Spread the sand along the base of the excavation, as this will help to bed the rail ties down and keep the base of the timber dry.

3 Next, you must decide on the lengths of your railroad ties. Measure them out and mark them for cutting.

4 You are now ready to cut your cross ties. A chain saw is the easiest tool for this job, but always wear protective clothing when using one.

5 Lay the ties in place to check their positions. Then move them to one side and dig a trench for each one to sit in.

6 Place the ties back in position and knock them down with a maul. Lay a straightedge from one side of the path to the other and along each tie, and check that the railroad tie finishes flush with the path edging.

7 Once all the railroad ties have been laid, turn the straightedge along the length of the path to ensure that the ties are all the same height. If any one of them is too high, it may cause someone to trip as they walk down the path. Adjust the heights as necessary.

Use the excavated hardcore to fill in along the edges of each rail tie and compact it with a handheld tamper. If you would like some sort of planting within the path, then this is the time to do it. Scrape out planting pockets within the hardcore and fill with topsoil. Then plant your selection of ground-cover plants.

8 Gravel can now be shoveled on and raked around the plants and between the railroad ties. You will need to rake gravel right up to the top of the ties and metal edging at first, but it will naturally settle in time to reveal the top edge of the ties. Gravel may range from $1/4$ in. to $3/4$ in., and the larger stones tend to move less. As a finishing touch to this natural design, position a few beach pebbles, available in bags from garden centers, in scattered groups around the clumps of plants. Choose natural colors for the gravel, such as limestone or slate chips.

Alternative materials

Some companies make small imitation railroad ties either 6 ft. or 3 ft. long, which are lighter and easier for one person to lift. They are machine-rounded, but they are flat on the top and bottom faces to make them easy to lay. Alternatively, you could use large 6 x 6 in. pressure-treated section timbers, which will give the look of rail ties but will be a lot cleaner.

For this particular project, we have chosen the crisp finish of a metal edge, but wood makes for an equally attractive edging material.

6 You can then place the cross ties back into position and bang them down to the correct height using a maul.

7 Once you have put all the ties in their final positions, use the straightedge to check that they are all at the same height.

8 Now you can put the gravel in the areas between your railroad ties. We have chosen to use fairly small gravel here.

boardwalk ACROSS WATER

On a warm summer's day, a boardwalk across water allows you to sit and enjoy the magical quality of a still, reflecting pool that mirrors the sky and trees while you dabble your toes in the cool water.

MATERIALS

Railroad ties

Wooden beams
3 × 6 × 36 in.

Ballast or sharp sand

Posts 2 × 2 in.

Deck slats 1½ × 5 in.

6-in. and 2½-in. galvanized nails

Wood stain

Chicken wire

Staples

TOOLS

Groundwork tools

Woodwork tools

Maul

Level

Aluminum ladder

Scaffold plank

String line

Paintbrush

Plastic sheet

1 Laying half a railroad tie at each end is the simplest base construction for a single-span boardwalk. First, decide on the finished height of the boardwalk above the water, not so high that it needs to be supported above ground level on the banks at either side, but if you are bridging a natural watercourse, high enough to cope with any changes in the water level. The underside of the proposed boardwalk beams will give you the finished height of the supporting railroad ties. Cut a tie in half to give you the support for each end of the boardwalk, then dig out a trench, allowing for the depth of the tie and a bed of ballast or sharp sand. Lay the first support and knock it down with a maul to the finished level. Using a level, check that it runs level across its length.

2 Excavate and lay the second support on the opposite bank. Then lay a wood beam across the water from one

1 Cut your tie to make two supports for either end of the boardwalk. Dig out a trench for the first and lay it in position.

2 Repeat for the second support. Check that the two are level by placing a beam across the water with a level on it.

KNOW YOUR MATERIALS

Decking boards are available in a variety of materials and widths, but treated softwood slats measuring 1½ x 5 in. are ideal. The wood is commonly available in 14-ft. lengths, which may then be cut by the supplier into four lengths of about 3 ft. each—this would make an ideal width for the boardwalk and will also save you from paying for wasted wood.

Before fixing the slats, it is a good idea to give them a coat of wood stain to protect against the elements, thereby extending the life expectancy of the wood. Stains are available in a range of different colors. Blue wood stain was used in this project to complement the effect of water.

support to the other, and use a level to check that the two supports are level. Knock the second support down with a maul until both are level. If it is not easy to gain access to the opposite bank to complete this stage, then you could lay an aluminum ladder and scaffold plank across from one side of the water to the other to act as a temporary bridge.

3 Fix the first beam in position by nailing through its side into the railroad tie support using a long galvanized nail. Check that it crosses the support at 90°, and fix the other end with a nail in the same manner. The beams need to be fairly substantial, so use 3 x 6 x 36 in. beams, which will probably require two people to carry them. Position the second beam parallel to the first one by measuring and checking that the space between the two beams is the same at each end. The width across from the outside of one beam to the outside of the other should allow for deck slats to overhang at each side by about 3 in.

4 The beams can then be firmly anchored by driving in long 2 x 2 in. posts. Drive them in with a beetle hard against the point inside the beams where the beams meet with the supports, driving them as far into the bank as they will go. Nail each post to both the beam and the support, and then cut off the post to a point just below the top of the beam.

5 Cut each of the deck slats to the same length. Nail one slat of decking board into position at each end of the boardwalk, then pull a string line taut between them along one edge. Now start to lay the rest of the deck slats, nailing them into position with one edge just touching the string line. Use a nail or a pencil as a spacer to leave a small gap of about 1/8 in. between each board. This gap is necessary to accommodate the natural expansion of the wood and to allow for better drainage of surface water. At this stage, only knock in one nail at each end of the board, and leave them raised in case you need to remove and realign any of the boards.

3 Fix each beam securely into its final position by using a long galvanized nail to attach it to the railroad tie support.

4 To firmly anchor each beam, you can drive a post into each of the corners where the beam meets the supports.

5 Begin to nail the boards into position. One edge of each board should align with the taut string line you have set up.

6 | Work your way across the water, nailing in boards in front of you as you go. When you have completed approximately half of the boardwalk, it is a good idea to lay out the remaining slats without nailing them down. This will tell you whether you need to increase or decrease the gap slightly between each board in order to fit all the boards neatly, without having to cut any of them down to a thin strip. If no adjustments are needed, fix nails at the end of each board so that they are all double-nailed at both ends. Once all the boards are fixed, check along the opposite edge to the string line to make sure that the ends there are all even, and if any are not, trim them with a panel saw and sand them to make them smooth.

7 | You will now need to check the entire boardwalk to see if you need to touch up any of the boards with stain, since cutting the boards may have resulted in some accidental removal of the stain. If restaining is needed, be sure to lay plastic over the water underneath to protect it from splashes, which would contaminate it.

8 | As a final touch, you may find it useful (especially if your boardwalk is positioned under trees) to tack chicken wire to the surface with staples. To do this, stretch the wire taut over the slats and curl it around the edges before fixing it down. This wire will not stand out too much and will help provide a good grip on the surface.

Alternative methods

Short areas of water can easily be spanned using large natural flagstones, perhaps sandstone or slate, whichever looks most appropriate. Railroad ties also work well, since they are solid, long-lasting, and require no complicated construction techniques, although two of them side by side are much safer than one. Stepping-stones may be used as a fun alternative if the water is wide enough. These could be paving slabs bedded onto concrete blocks or natural boulders bedded at the base of the pool. For a wider span, a galvanized steel walkway could be used in a high-tech design, or decking slats secured to solid wood beams may form an extension to an existing wood deck.

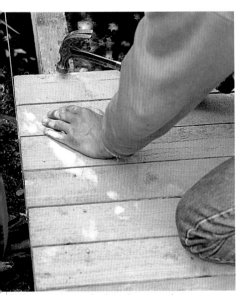

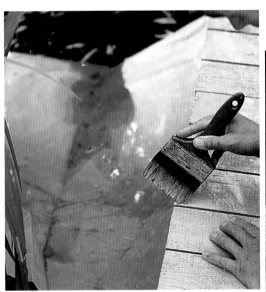

6 Continue laying the boards across the water. Be careful as you do this—take your time and nail the board in front of you as you go.

7 Having laid a plastic sheet on the water under the board, paint any areas of the boardwalk that need to be touched up.

8 To protect your boardwalk and to provide a good grip on the surface, you may want to fix chicken wire to the boards.

granite and GRAVEL PATH

Patterned pathways make attractive, eye-catching garden features. Materials such as cobblestones, bricks, and setts are ideal for intricate designs, or you could experiment by combining granite with different textures such as grass or gravel.

1 | Mark out the position of the path according to your plan. Dig to a depth of approximately 6 in., which allows for a 4-in.-deep sett and 2 in. of mortar or concrete.

It is important to plan the dimensions of the pattern before you begin so that you end up with a regular pattern when you start to lay the stones. To achieve this pattern, you need to allow 40 in. between the corners of each diamond. Lay out a section of the path dry to see how the pattern works and to establish the correct width of the path.

2 | When you are satisfied with the layout, you can start to lay one of the path edges. First, set up a string line to indicate the finished height and the line of the path. It is impossible to create two absolutely neat edges with a material such as granite setts, so position your line on the inside of the path edge, because this is the side of the

MATERIALS

Granite setts: 4 x 4 x 4 in.

Mortar

Hardcore

Gravel

TOOLS

Groundwork tools

Paving tools

1 Lay out a section of the diamond pattern dry so that you can determine the correct dimensions for the width of the path.

2 Use a club hammer to tap down the setts along the path edges. Use a stiff mortar mix and leave ³/₈ in. between each sett.

KNOW YOUR MATERIALS

Granite setts: The natural appearance and hard-wearing surface of stone setts lend a sense of permanence to any garden. Of all the natural stone setts, granite is the most durable and most commonly used in urban settings, where it is often laid in a fan pattern or with cobblestones for roadways. One benefit of using granite setts for a garden path is that because they are so solid, they do not need to be bedded down on a layer of hardcore. Simply bind the setts with mortar to prevent any movement.

Shingle: With its warm color, shingle is just what is needed to break up the hardness of granite setts, and also provides a crunchy textured surface.

setts that will always be visible; the outer edge of the path will be covered with plants or turf. Make a stiff 1:6 mortar mix and trowel out the mortar to form a full bed alongside the string line. Position the setts in the mortar, and tap them down with a club hammer until the tops rest level with the string line. Leave a joint of about ³⁄₈ in. between each sett, although the joints will vary because of the uneven edges of the stone.

Measure across to the other edge of the path and repeat the whole process. Once again, remember to position the string line on the inside edge of the setts. Do not try to match up these setts with those in the opposite edge. This is not possible given the irregularity of the setts and would result in joints that are too wide.

3 Next, lay a row of setts as a header row at the end of the path to connect the two side edges.

Pack the outside edges of the header row and the edging setts with stiff mortar mix, applying the mortar up to just below the tops of the setts. This is done to support the edges from any side-to-side movement that might otherwise occur. If your pathway is to have a lot of heavy use, then pack the edging setts with concrete rather than mortar in order to make them stronger.

4 When the edges are complete, once again lay a short section of the path pattern dry to double-check the design. Move the setts around until the pattern is just right and all the sides of the diamonds are equal and properly lined up. Now mark the setts along each edging with a chalk or pencil mark at 40-in. intervals to indicate where the points of the diamonds will touch the sides along the length of the path. You may need to adjust the space between each sett in the diamond to ensure that the diamond points and pencil marks match up.

5 Remove the dry-laid setts and start to lay a bed of stiff 1:6 mortar mix. Tie a central string line along the length of the path to help center the diamond pattern. However, if you find that this hinders the laying process, then remove

3 To keep path edges stable, spread a layer of mortar or concrete along the outside edges to just below the tops of the setts.

4 Lay out the pattern again to check that it fits, and mark the edge setts with a pencil where the diamond points touch the sides.

5 Use a club hammer to tap the setts into position in the mortar bed. Tie a string line along the path to help center the pattern.

it, because it is not essential. Begin to bed the setts back in position, laying mortar only as you need it and only under the setts, leaving the other areas empty. Tap the setts down with a club hammer. Continue to lay the rest of the pattern. As you go, use a straightedge to ensure that all the setts line up neatly and finish flush across the top with the two edges of the pathway.

6 Before topping up the path to the finished level with gravel, it is important to point the setts with a fairly crumbly 1:4 mortar mix. You could use a weaker mix, such as 1:6 (the same as that used for the bedding), because this will allow mosses to grow, which always look good in a garden setting. Push the mortar down well into the joints using a brick trowel before giving them a rubbed finish.

7 The following day, place hardcore in the areas between the diamond patterns. Do not attempt to do this any earlier in the process, otherwise you will risk dislodging the setts. Bring the hardcore to just below the top of the setts and compact it down with a handheld tamper to form a solid base for the gravel to be placed on.

8 Wait until the pointing has set completely to avoid damaging the mortar, before spreading the gravel. Simply shovel the gravel from a wheelbarrow and spread it between the setts to complete the path surface. You will need a maximum depth of approximately 1 in. to create a firm surface to walk on.

Alternative materials

All types of aggregates can be used for the surface in patterned paths such as this. Granite chips will blend with the granite setts, producing a subtly contrasting finish, whereas wood chips will lend a more rustic character to the pathway. Or, simply lay grass to really blend the path with the garden, although this will only be appropriate for a path used less frequently; otherwise, the path may become scuffed and muddy in wet weather.

6 Point the setts with a crumbly mortar mix. Use a brick trowel to press the mortar down well between the joints.

7 Let sit for a day; apply the hardcore between the setts, up to just below the tops of the stones. Compact with a handheld tamper.

8 Finally, shovel the gravel into position between the setts. Fill to a maximum depth of 1 in. to make the surface firm.

straight brick path
WITH CORNER

The warm colors of clay bricks blend well with many other natural colors, while their angular shape is particularly suited for creating a path to complement an orderly, geometric-style garden.

1 | Work out the path position from the plan and excavate for the base (see pages 26–7), allowing 3 in. for the hardcore and 3 in. for the depth of the bricks and sand bed.

Spread the hardcore over the base and compact it down. Then set up a string line along one edge of the path to indicate the line and finished height of the path, which should be flush with the level of any adjacent lawn or beds. Lay a tightly jointed line of stretcher bricks on a bed of mortar, and tap them down to the line. These edging bricks will give strength to the path by holding the dry-laid bricks tightly together in place, preventing any side-to-side movement.

2 | Support the line of edging bricks by packing them on the outside edge with a strong 1:6 mortar mix using sharp sand, or even a concrete mix of the same strength. The

MATERIALS

Hardcore

Sharp sand

Kiln-dried sand

Cement

Paving-quality bricks

TOOLS

Groundwork tools

Paving tools

Plate compactor

Screeding board

1 Lay a row of stretcher bricks along one of the path's edges to make the path strong and to provide support for the dry-laid bricks.

2 Pack the outside of the brick edging with mortar or concrete to hold the bricks firmly in place.

KNOW YOUR MATERIALS

The small unit size of bricks is ideal for laying a wide variety of surface patterns, especially curves, with the added benefit that they require no excessive cutting. Many paving bricks are now manufactured as true rectangles—4 × 8 in.—which enables patterns such as basket-weave to be completed without the need for jointing. A wide range of paving bricks is available, so you will always be able to find one type that harmonizes with the house or the garden walls. Also consider how the bricks will look set against existing plant beds or any plantings you have planned. Try to avoid concrete paving bricks, which look unnatural and tend to fade.

mortar or concrete should finish just below the top edge of the bricks to allow soil or turf to finish flush with the paving.

3 It is possible to mark out the opposite edge of the path simply by measuring, but a safer method is to lay out the exact number of bricks across the width of the path, including the edging brick, in order to locate the true edge position. Remember to butt the bricks, as there will be no joints. This should be done at both ends of the path so that when a line is set up, it runs parallel with the opposite path edge.

4 Lay the second edge of stretcher bricks in the same manner as the first, and pack the outside edge with mortar. You can then lay the header course of bricks that will form the end of the path in mortar. Pack the outside edge of these header bricks, as well. These bricks can either be laid flat, as shown here, or on edge, which would necessitate the removal of some of the hardcore. The edging bricks

and the header course need to be left overnight to set firm before you proceed, otherwise they might be pushed out of position when you lay the paving bricks.

5 The next day, spread a thin layer of sand between the two path edges and screed it level with a screeding board. Cut this board from a piece of wood to fit over the edges of the path, so that it is deep enough to leave just the right amount of bedding. Ideally, the sand should be compacted to remove any soft spots and then dressed with another layer, which should be screeded so that the sand finishes approximately 1/4 in. up the inside edges of the path.

6 Position two or three rows of paving bricks into the sand along one edge in a running-bond pattern. Remember that alternate bricks in the first row next to the header course will need to be cut in half to start off the bonding pattern. Tap the bricks down into place. Lay a block of wood (you could use the screeding board) from edge to edge and tap it down so that the bricks finish flush across

3 The safest way to measure the width of the path is to lay the exact number of bricks in position, including the edging brick.

4 Lay a header course of bricks at one end of the path and leave to dry overnight until the bricks have set firmly.

5 Spread a thin layer of sand between the path edges and use a screed board to level out the sand.

the width. On a long pathway, you could use a plate compactor to knock the bricks into position, but always stop about 40 in. from the laying edge to avoid loosening the bricks and the screeded bed. Continue laying bricks along the length of the path until you reach the far side of the first corner, taking care not to walk on the screeded sand.

7 In this project, the corners are made by butting each subsequent stretch of path along a straight joint with the previous stretch. Start the running bond for the next stretch of path with alternate half bricks as before. Continue to build the right-angled stretches of path in this way according to your plan.

8 When all the bricks have been laid, brush kiln-dried sand into the surface in order to seal the joints and help bind all the bricks together. Do not worry if some of the sand is left on the surface, as this will freely wash down into any gaps the next time it rains. If the joints are slightly open, then some additional, grittier sharp sand can also be brushed in.

Alternative methods

Instead of creating corners with a straight joint across the path, the same running bond could turn the corner with a herringbone miter, which does not require any cutting. Patterns like herringbone and basket-weave are best suited to traditional-style gardens, whereas a grid pattern creates a more contemporary feel.

You could also lay bricks as a rigid construction—on a mortar bed with all the joints mortar-pointed. This will look very smart and will be in keeping with a traditional garden, but the pointing makes this method time-consuming. It is far quicker to lay bricks butt jointed on a bed of compacted sand, as has been shown here. This is ideal for long garden paths where excessive pointing might otherwise be required. However it is always best to use crisp-edged bricks to maintain a tight joint.

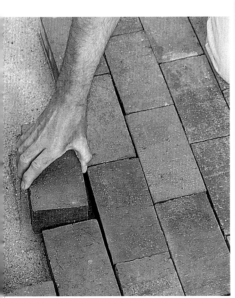

6 Lay the bricks in a running-bond pattern, fixing the units firmly in place in the sand before tapping them in.

7 One way of making a 90° corner in a path is to create a straight joint and then cut half-bricks to fit the turn in the pattern.

8 To seal the joints and bind the bricks together, brush kiln-dried sand into the surface of the path.

curved SETT PATH

Disappearing behind a riot of colorful plants, this curved path made from granite setts adds a sense of mystery and discovery to a simple walk around the garden.

1 | Mark out the path and drive in timber pegs to indicate both curved edges and the finished height of the path. Tie a string line onto the pegs for this purpose. In this project, the height of the path has been adjusted at intervals, by a simple step of one sett's height, to accommodate an existing gradient. Excavate down, allowing a 4-in. depth for the setts, 1½ in. for mortar, and 3 in. for the hardcore. Spread the hardcore and compact it down to the correct level with a handheld tamper, or use a plate compactor for a long pathway.

2 | Make up a fairly dry mix of 1:6 mortar. Trowel it out on top of the hardcore, just along the length of the outer edge of the path. Lay the edge setts on the mortar following the approximate curve of the string line, although you will have to adjust the position of the setts by eye to achieve a true curve. Continue until you

MATERIALS

Wood pegs

Hardcore

String

Mortar

Granite setts

Wood

TOOLS

Groundwork tools

Paving tools

Watering can

1 Mark your path with timber pegs and a line of string attached to them. This will serve as an edge, as well as indicating the finished height.

2 Lay mortar around the outer edge and place the edge setts into it. You can use the string as a guide for the curve.

KNOW YOUR MATERIALS

Reclaimed granite setts look robust and have a timeless quality. The setts in this project are fairly evenly sized cubes measuring approximately 4 × 4 × 4 in. Longer rectangular setts are also available, which are useful for making irregular patterns. Setts will usually be slightly tapered, and the smallest face of the sett should be laid on the mortar, with the other end forming the surface of the path. You can often see some old mortar still stuck to the base of secondhand setts, which will help you choose the correct face. You could also use new setts, but they are expensive and will take time to weather and lose their raw appearance.

complete the edge, and pack the outside of the setts with mortar to hold them firmly in position.

3 You can now determine the position of the inside edge of the path. The best way to do this is to lay a line of setts out dry, with spaces for mortar joints, across the beginning of the proposed path to establish the accurate width. Then cut a length of wood to this same width to use as a gauge or spacer when laying the inside edging of the path.

4 Lay the final row of setts with mortar and then proceed with the inside edge. Use the wood spacer across the width of the path to ensure that the width is consistent down the length. Start by laying out an approximately 40-in. run of edging by eye, and then tap the setts into their exact position after you have used the spacer to double-check their width. Do not try to line up the setts on the inside edge with corresponding ones on the outside; on the inner edge of a curved line this will be impossible. Continue laying the edging setts to the end of

the path until the run is complete. Again, pack the outside of this line of setts with mortar to hold them firm.

5 You can now lay the main surface of the path on a bed of mortar. The easiest method is to lay lines, or "runs," of setts along the length of the path, following the curve of the edges. Again, do not expect the setts and joints to line up across the path. If you try to lay setts across the width, it will be difficult to avoid opening up large joints against the edge as you work around the outside of the curve. You will also find that the setts get too tight against the edge on the inside of a curve, so work systematically lengthways.

6 Work your way down the path in "runs" of about 6 ft. before starting the next line of setts. Continue in this manner until you have covered the entire length of the first section. Start off again laying lines for another 6-ft. section, and repeat until all the setts have been laid. As you approach the end of the path, you may have to adjust some of the joints to ensure that you complete the path

3 Lay the end row of setts out dry before bedding them in mortar; use this measure to establish the correct width of the path.

4 Use a piece of wood that is cut to equal the width between the two edges as a gauge for laying the inside edge of the path.

5 The rest of the path can now be laid. It is much easier to do this lengthwise rather than across the width.

with whole setts—without having to try cutting any setts and without leaving excessively large mortar joints.

The setts can be laid almost completely by hand, as they only need the occasional tap down with a club hammer to level them off. However, to make sure that all the setts are level when a section of paving has been laid, place a piece of wood across from edge to edge and tap down with a club hammer. If you do not work in manageable sections but continue laying individual lines to the end of the path, you will find that the first setts in the line will have set firm before you have a chance to tap them down.

When laying reclaimed setts, as we have here, you should make sure that the best face is on the surface, not the one that was previously bedded in mortar. If all or some of the setts that you are using are wedge-shaped, the narrow part of the wedge should be the face that is laid into the mortar.

7 After laying all the setts, prepare a dry mix of mortar at 1:4 (or 1:6 for a slightly lighter appearance). Spread the

dry mortar over the setts and work it into the joints with a brush. You must make sure that the mortar is brushed in well to avoid staining the surface of the setts.

8 When all the mortar has been properly worked in, lightly water the surface of the path using a watering can with a sprinkler attachment. Do not use a hose or a watering can without a sprinkler, because the strong stream of water will wash the mix out of the joints and stain the setts. A light watering will produce a slightly recessed joint and give good definition to the edge of the setts.

Alternative materials

Reclaimed sandstone setts offer a warmer alternative to granite. They are supplied either as diamond-sawed setts, which have crisp edges, or as tumbled setts, which have the edges rounded off for a more weathered appearance.

There are also some excellent imitation setts, manufactured in precast concrete, which are laid on a sand bed and then vibrated into place with a plate compactor.

6 Continue down the path, placing 6-ft. runs of setts at a time. Make sure each run of setts is level before laying additional runs.

7 Once the path is laid, you should prepare a dry mortar mix that will then be worked into each of the joints.

8 When all the mortar is in place, lightly water the surface to recess the joints and clean off any excess mortar.

edgings and trims

planning for edgings and trims

Although often similar in appearance and construction, edgings may be functional—whether retaining a flexible surface such as gravel or serving as a mowing edge to reduce maintenance—or purely decorative, in the form of bricks laid flush along the edge of a patio. The lines between the two sometimes become blurred, and in many cases, a functional edging may also become a decorative trim.

Function and style The main purpose of edgings is to retain a flexible surface. They often act as miniature retaining walls, holding back soil in flower beds or vegetable plots from adjacent paths. Mowing edges are installed to fulfill another important function—to avoid laborious trimming where a firm brick edge is set flush with a lawn. This same type of edge can also be laid where lawn is next to a wall, again for ease of mowing. If a paving slab is used for this purpose, on the other hand, the edge also becomes a pathway, enabling easy access to house windows for maintenance. Wide strips such as this may also be installed simply because the ground is often so dry in this position that nothing will grow. If the walls of the house are rendered or in pale brick, then gravel may be laid as a maintenance strip, rather than slabs, so that there is no splash back onto the walls. Gravel strips can also act as areas for catching water from gutterless roofs and then as a reservoir for irrigation systems.

Although not always highly visible, it is important to get the detail of edgings and trims just right, as they must look good with the style of paving that they border and form a common link with other materials in the garden. An obvious example is to use brick rather than granite setts as an edge to a gravel path if bricks have been used elsewhere. In the same way, it would be wrong to choose a bland concrete edging instead of the traditional rope-top edging in a Victorian-style kitchen garden.

Design choices Edgings must be fit for their purpose; for example, wood path edgings are normally a minimum of 1 in. thick, as anything thinner would bend and break. Timber of this thickness can be bent around curves by making saw cuts on one face. Thicker timbers of perhaps

Slate surrounded by setts.

Metal edging against a stained deck.

Large pebbles laid against smaller aggregates.

A colorfully stained wood edge.

Edgings and trims can perform a functional or decorative purpose, or serve both. An informal arrangement of dark stones helps to retain a loose aggregate pathway (top left), while a pyramid of metal planters fulfills the same function between plants and a lawn (top right). A border of bricks along a pathway of paving slabs, however, is purely decorative, as the box hedging performs the function of containing the planting (above).

Basket-weave edging enhances the country-cottage feel of a profusion of colorful, cottage-style plants.

2–3 in. may be used on straight runs to form a much more obvious neat trim along the side of a path. Cost will also have an influence on design choices. For example, curved edges can be cheaply and quickly installed using treated wood boards; bricks or setts may look much better, retaining the character of the garden, but they are slower to lay and much more costly in terms of materials.

Types of edgings and trims
Pressure-treated path edging is readily available, can be laid to curves, and when secured to driven wood pegs, is easy to install. It can be used to edge pathways of loose aggregate, such as gravel or wood chips, and may also be used as a temporary edging with mortar-bedded bricks. As a permanent edging to sand-bedded bricks, wood boards that are about 3 in. wide look good and are in the correct proportion to the width of the bricks. Logs laid along the edge of a pathway in a woodland setting are attractive and may help to retain soil banks, but they act more as a trim in defining the path than as a functional edging. Bricks are probably the ideal edging unit, because they provide a link with

> *Bricks are commonly laid as mowing edges; they also form the ideal trim for paving.*

bricks used elsewhere in the garden and are easy to lay in curves. Bricks are commonly laid as mowing edges; they also form the ideal trim for paving. They can also be run as lines through a patio for a purely decorative effect. Concrete path edgings are often best suited to pavements, rather than garden paths. The simple flat-topped concrete path edging can be used effectively as a mowing edge, but only along straight lines. There are some excellent imitation setts in precast concrete, which are effective as pathways, but they can also bring continuity to a garden when used as edgings. Paving slabs can also be laid to form a mowing edge. You can position slabs around curved lawns without cutting them by opening up wide joints between them that can be laid to turf. A lawn mower can then easily pass over the slabs to mow the grass without any need for edging shears. Natural stone flags will serve the same purpose as paving slabs, while sandstone or granite setts may be bedded on concrete and laid to curves to form a hard-wearing edge. Large pebbles or small boulders look good when laid as a decorative trim to pathways of smaller aggregates. Metal strips, available in 40-in. lengths, are easy to install and provide a crisp edge to lawns.

Plants can be surrounded successfully by a whole host of edgings that create different moods. Old wood boards set on their sides enhance an informal planting that is complemented by colorful slate chips (above left). For a more traditional look, bricks positioned in a herringbone pattern at the edge of a path (above right) act as an edging to the delightfully scented flowers in the bed beside it.

Pebbles form a decorative trim.

A run of decorative bricks forms a perfect trim.

Metal edging finishes off this unusual pathway.

Clay pipes on bricks make a raised bed edging.

timber EDGING

Timber edging is one of the simplest types of edging to lay. As well as combating soil and path erosion, timber can look very attractive. There is a wide range of wood stains available, or you might even prefer the natural wood effect. For a different look, you could try metal edging, which would complement a contemporary garden.

1 | Timber edging can be used for either straight or curved paths. To bend the wood, lay a length out flat over a couple of pegs or battens that have been placed on the ground for support. Cut out notches with a panel saw, about 2 in. apart, along one face of the board.

Mark out the position of the path according to your plan, knocking in pointed wood pegs at intervals of about 40 in. along the length of each edge line.

Set the timber edgings to the inside (path side) of the pegs, tapping them down with a club hammer so that the edging sits just below lawn level. Fix the timber edging to the pegs with galvanized nails. For a curved path, position the timbers so that the notched edge is on the inside of the curve. For a neat finish, bend the middle—rather than the end—of the boards around the pegs.

2 | Join together the lengths of path edging by cutting a separate short section of edging, and butt the two ends

MATERIALS
Timber path edging: 1 in. × 4 in. × 12 ft.

Wood pegs: 2 × 2 × 18 in.

Galvanized nails

Spiked metal edging strips

TOOLS
Groundwork tools

Woodwork tools

Club hammer

Block of wood

1 For a curved path, make a series of notches about halfway through the timber at intervals of approximately 2 in.

2 When the boards are in position, saw the pegs down so that they are level with the edging, and treat the cut ends.

KNOW YOUR MATERIALS

Timber path edging: This is usually treated softwood, available in 12-ft. lengths of 1 x 4 in. sawed timber. Once cut, the timber can be stained or left natural.

Metal edgings: These come in short sections about 12 in. long and are available in various decorative patterns. Long sections of flat galvanized steel are also available in 40-in. lengths. Easy to cut and bend, metal edgings can be used for both straight lines and curves. Though they are often painted in earth tones, they could just as easily be left in their original metallic state.

against it. Then nail the three pieces together with galvanized nails to create the join. By doing this, you avoid having to nail two ends of edging to one peg; instead, you can arrange to fix pegs to the middle of the edging boards, which will result in a much neater finish.

Once the boards have been fixed into position in the ground, saw the pegs down to the top of the boards and treat the cut ends.

Metal edging

1 | Cut a clean edge to the turf or shrub bed before knocking the spiked metal edge into position with a club hammer and a block of wood.

2 | Butt one length of edging up against the next one and knock it down as before. Continue in this way along the line until the edge is complete.

Metal edging: *Silver galvanized metal edging looks good here as an edge to the blue-gray slate path.*

toothed brick EDGING

Toothed brick edging can be used to create an ornamental, patterned trim for any path or patio, but it also fulfills the practical function of retaining loose materials.

1 First, decide on the overall height above path level by which the edging needs to protrude in order to retain the adjacent soil. Ideally, this will be at least 3 in. to best show off the decorative style of the edging. A string line can now be set up along the length of the path to indicate the finished height.

Next, excavate a trench along the side of the path to a depth that allows for approximately two-thirds of the brick to be below the finished path level, taking into account a 2-in. bed of concrete. A mattock is a useful tool for excavating the trench; the trench does not need to be very wide.

2 Make a stiff 1:6 concrete or mortar mix using sharp sand. Trowel the mix into the trench, and push the bricks into it so that the top corner of each brick touches the string line. Position the first brick at a 60° angle, and the rest will follow. Continue to lay the bricks, butting them tightly

MATERIALS

Well-fired paving bricks

Concrete or stiff mortar mix using sharp sand

TOOLS

Groundwork tools

Paving tools

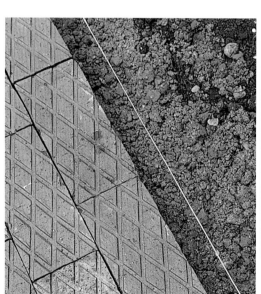

1 Determine the planned height of the brick edging above path level and set up a string line to indicate this height.

2 Set the bricks at a 60° angle in mortar. Use a club hammer to tap them down so that their top edge is just touching the string line.

KNOW YOUR MATERIALS

Bricks may be used to edge paths in many different ways: laid flat, on edge, as stretchers (laid lengthwise), and as headers (laid widthwise). They are often mortared into place, where they form an edge restraint to paths of sand-bedded bricks. In these instances, the edging does not stand out but finishes flush to form an integral part of the path. For this project, however, a toothed edge is created by laying the bricks vertically and at an angle. This style of edging is often used to retain the soil in vegetable gardens, but it should not be used against lawns, because it is impossible to mow up to or over.

together without a joint. If necessary, tap them with a club hammer until they touch the string line.

3 Once you have completed a line of bricks about 6 ft. in length, you can pack concrete behind them to hold them firmly in place. If the edging is laid before the path, pack concrete on both sides of the brick, keeping it low on the inside to allow for the depth of the surfacing material. If you are laying a pathway of loose aggregate, where the edging is used to keep the path material in place, the brick edge should be laid first. With a solid path, however, the edging can be constructed after the paving is laid, as it does not form part of the path construction.

Continue laying bricks and packing them in until the line is complete. Finish by backfilling soil over the concrete behind the bricks.

3 When the bricks are in place and have been packed with mortar, backfill over the concrete behind the bricks with soil.

mowing EDGE

Where two different areas of the garden meet, why not set them off and make an ornamental feature with merging lines of curved brick edging?

1 | Using sand or spray paint, mark out a general line for the first set of edging on the ground. Excavate a trench about a spade's width and to a depth that allows for 3 in. of concrete and an additional 3 in. for the depth of the bricks on a mortar bed.

Drive in timber pegs approximately 40 in. apart around the outside of the concrete foundation to indicate the finished height and to show the general line the edging should follow. However, it is impossible to set a string line to a curve. Instead, the bricks must be carefully laid to a curve by eye.

There is no need for mortar if you are laying a short run of edging, as you can push the bricks straight into the concrete before it sets. On a longer run, however, you will need to lay the bricks into a bed of mortar (1:6 mix), otherwise the concrete will set hard before you have a chance to push all the bricks down. Wait until the concrete sets before laying the mortar bed.

MATERIALS

Pegs

Concrete

Mortar

Paving-quality bricks

String

TOOLS

Groundwork tools

Paving tools

Slab cutter

1 Use the guide pegs and string to place your first line of bricks at the right height. The smooth curve will have to be done by eye.

2 Where two lines converge, you will need to cut the bricks to size. Raise them up to mark where they need to be cut.

KNOW YOUR MATERIALS

The key idea behind a mowing edge is that it should be flat enough to be easily mown over, which avoids the need for laborious edge trimming. It is therefore essential that the edging is laid as evenly as possible and that none of the bricks or slabs stand up above the height of the lawn. Bricks are an ideal material for constructing a mowing edge, because their small unit size makes them perfect for laying to the curved lines of a lawn. In this particular project, paving bricks have been used to form a neat link with those that have been used elsewhere in the garden.

3 Once the bricks are pointed and packed in, remove any mortar and concrete from the middle so it is ready for the grass to be sown.

2 | To make the two lines of edging converge, lay the outside line of edging in the same way as the inside until the two meet. At this point, the bricks will need to be cut to fit. Take the first brick to be cut and position it on the correct line but raised up and supported by a spare brick underneath, so that it overlaps the inside line of bricks. Mark with a pencil on the brick where the outer edge of the inside line of bricks will come to. Use a slab cutter to cut along this pencil line. Repeat as necessary.

3 | When all the bricks have been laid, point them up either with the same mortar mix or a slightly stronger mix, and finish with a rubbed joint. The outside of each brick line should be packed with concrete to hold it in place. However, scrape out the mortar and concrete between the two lines of brick in order to provide a sufficient depth of topsoil for the grass to grow properly.

rock EDGE

Not all edging requires complicated construction techniques—a relaxed look can be achieved simply by laying down an informal edge of rocks and pebbles.

1 First, decide on the line of the edging. There is no need to set up a string line for this project, because the edging will look better if an uneven effect is created in which the tops of the rocks are not all level.

Next, dig out a shallow trench for the rocks. No great depth of excavation is necessary, but the rocks will look better if they are partially buried rather than perched on the surface.

Now select and arrange the rocks. Rocks are too heavy to keep shifting from place to place, so it is worthwhile to take your time and carefully select those that will look just right the first time around. If you are working close to water or in a boggy area, it can be awkward trying to move rocks around by hand—a few shovelfuls of hardcore spread around the area will ease movement considerably.

If the ground is at all stony, it can be difficult to bed down the heavy boulders. Spread a shovelful of sharp

MATERIALS

Rounded boulders

Beach pebbles

Sharp sand

Hardcore

TOOLS

Groundwork tools

Club hammer

Trowel

Handheld tamper

1 Select your rocks and lay them onto a bed of sharp sand—make ridges and furrows in the sand to make it easier to work the rocks down.

2 Spread out mixed pebbles across the hardcore base to create a reasonably flat surface and even mix of pebbles.

3 Once the pebbles and rocks are in position,
shovel soil in behind them and ram this in with
a club hammer to set the rocks in place.

sand under each rock to ease the process. Push the sand
around with a trowel to create ridges and furrows into
which the boulder can be worked down.

2 After all the rocks have been placed and the soil packed
in, ram down hardcore in front of the rocks and over the
width of the proposed path, or "beach" area, to form a
firm base. Open up the bags of mixed pebbles and spread
them evenly over the hardcore base, pushing the pebbles
around by hand. The aim should be to achieve a
reasonably flat surface and an even mix of the different-
sized pebbles.

3 When you are happy with the pebble surface and the
position of each rock, shovel in soil behind the rocks. This
soil can then be rammed in with a club hammer to help
hold the smaller rocks in place.

steps

planning for steps

Steps provide access from one part of the garden to another where a path or patio meets a change in level. The mood of the garden will be reflected in the style of the steps: stone flags and paving slab treads link well with patios that are made out of the same types of material in the ordered areas of the garden close to the house. Log risers and treads of wood chips, on the other hand, are more suited to the relaxed, wooded areas farther away.

Function and style A flight of steps may be purely functional, providing quick direct access, possibly in a utility area or perhaps up from the front door to the garage. A raised terrace will require steps down into the garden, while a patio cut into a bank will need steps up through the retaining walls for access. Even a flat site will need steps, if only out from the house and down onto the patio. Interest could be added to a flat site by constructing a seating area that is raised above ground level, again requiring a step up for access.

Steps should certainly reflect the mood of the garden and relate to other materials that have been used. It makes sense to lead on and off the patio with steps that have treads of the same slabs that have been used for the rest of the paving. Bricks that have been used in the terrace retaining walls should also follow through into the step risers. When moving away from the harder areas of construction close to the house, the style of steps may reflect the more relaxed parts of the garden farther away. In these areas, wood is the usual choice, because it blends well with the more natural landscape and is often used to form the step risers with treads of gravel or wood chips.

Design choices Steps designed for quick access tend to be quite narrow with a shallow depth of tread, while broader steps will encourage a gentler ascent where speed is not of the essence. Staggering a flight of steps up a bank creates far more interest than a straight flight, which is often too grand for most gardens anyway. Curved steps or those that have a change in angle are also inviting, and along with staggered steps, they are far easier to soften and partially obscure with plants, a feat that is impossible with a straight flight.

Curved wood decking steps.

Natural stone and pebbles.

Gray stone steps.

Stone slabs and brick risers.

It is important that the style of steps you choose matches the mood of your garden. Curved steps with wood risers and gravel treads (top left) fit well in the cottage garden with lots of overhanging plants partially obscuring the steps. Similarly, the wild nature of the stone steps covered in ivy (above) is perfect in this natural-style garden. On the other hand, the clean, crisp lines of the broad curved steps (top right) complement the ordered style of the herbaceous borders nearby.

Weathered, broad stone steps covered in wild, informal green plants.

The character of the steps will also be affected by their edge treatment. They may have sidewalls for a sharp appearance, or on the other hand, they may be planted at the sides for a softer, more relaxed look.

Well-designed steps will have a comfortable balance between tread depth and riser height, and for safety reasons, the risers should be the same size for the entire flight. A broad, deep tread or landing can be planned halfway up a long flight of steps, where a bench may be positioned at which to rest and take a breather. Shadow lines, where the tread overhangs the riser, will hide the mortar joint and give a clear definition to each step, while carefully positioned lights will illuminate the steps for safety and make them look inviting when darkness falls.

Step materials Extending the path or patio material on into the steps provides a strong continuity of design. To this end, treads are commonly laid in paving slabs, while the risers may be constructed from bricks used elsewhere in the garden. An alternative riser in traditional steps can be made from thin slates bedded horizontally with no

Steps should reflect the mood of the garden and relate to other materials that have been used.

visible mortar. This detail looks good with sandstone or slate flagstones for the treads.

Bricks are frequently used in the garden for walls, edgings, and paths, so it follows that they should also be used to form steps. The bricks must be well-fired, hard bricks to withstand frost. They may be laid either flat or on edge, and can be used to form both the riser and the tread. They are commonly laid in a running-bond pattern across the width, thus making the steps seem wider and encouraging a gentle ascent, while bricks laid from front to back will tend to make the steps seem narrower and encourage quicker movement.

Sawed wooden slats can be used to make box-shaped steps, which blend well with raised decks, while larger sections of timber or even railroad ties may be used for more informal steps in woodland areas with treads of gravel or wood chips. Log rounds work well in similar locations, forming simple steps up through a wooded bank. A combination of materials can be very effective, using one type for the riser and another for the tread. Railroad ties and other solid timber sections look superb as risers with treads of brick or granite setts. As an alternative to timber risers, large blocks of granite or sandstone can also be effective.

Stone slabs can be used to create a variety of effects. They can have a formal appearance, such as the short flight of broad stone steps (above left) punctuated by containers and surrounded by lush herbaceous borders, which encourage walkers to take their time as they move up or down. Stone slabs can also have an informal appearance, such as the curved steps in a seaside setting (above right), made out of slabs with uneven edges.

Straight timber decking steps.

Weathered stone.

Brick treads and risers.

Stone treads and terra-cotta tile risers.

railroad tie STEPS

The long treads of this flight of railroad tie steps encourage gentle strolling, while the combination of sturdy ties and crunchy slate chips also makes for a pretty and inviting seat. Try fixing candleholders along the rise for instant ambience on a warm evening.

1 | Measure from the top to the bottom of the bank and calculate the number of steps required, taking into account the height of the risers and depth of each tread. Long treads were possible on this relatively shallow slope and were most appropriate for a stroll through woodland. Next, excavate for the first riser at the bottom of the slope and spread a thin layer of ballast on which to bed the railroad tie. Two people will be needed to lift the tie, as it will be extremely heavy and awkward to handle. Lay the bottom tie in position on its edge and hammer it into the ground so that about 3–4 in. is buried, leaving a riser of 6–7 in.

2 | Having laid the first riser, and with the top level of the flight of steps already established, you can now roughly excavate the bank to shape. Cut the ground back from the first riser to behind the proposed second riser

MATERIALS

Railroad ties

Ballast

Pegs

Galvanized nails

Hardcore

Soil

Slate chips

Grass seed

TOOLS

Groundwork tools

Maul or sledgehammer

Level

Tamper

1 Once you have excavated the space for the first riser and placed a layer of ballast on it, put the railroad tie in position.

2 Continue cutting the steps out of the bank, placing a wood peg to indicate the top level of each step.

KNOW YOUR MATERIALS

Slate chips: These chips are especially effective, because their blue color contrasts well with the railroad ties, and they possess the rare quality of looking even better when wet.

Old railroad ties: These are tough and uncompromising but are actually easy to install, needing no concrete footings or mortar bedding. Ties are readily available either new or as secondhand materials. New ones are cleaner but more

expensive. Railroad ties can normally be purchased in dimensions of 6 in. × 9 in. × 8 ft.. They are available as Grade I or Grade II. Grade I uses the best condition wood with very few twists or bows.

position, then continue doing the same for the rest of the steps up the bank. When digging out, allow for a depth of approximately 2 in. to be excavated for each tread in order to make enough room for hardcore and loose aggregate. As you work up the bank, drive in a wood peg at one end of each level to indicate the finished height of each step. If you position them just outside where the railroad tie will sit, these same pegs can be used to hold the ties in position.

3 After the rough excavation has been completed and all the level pegs are in position, you are now ready to set the second railroad tie in place. Scrape out a shallow trench and spread a thin layer of ballast over it to provide a firm base for the tie. Use a maul or sledgehammer to knock the sleeper down to the height of the adjacent level peg.

4 Be sure that the railroad tie riser is level along its length with a level, and knock it down slightly, if necessary. This

process of bedding the ties on ballast, knocking them down to their peg, and then leveling along their length should be continued up the entire length of the bank until all the risers have been laid.

5 Once all the risers have been laid in position, drive in two wood pegs on the front face of each riser (apart from the first one), just in from each end. You can reuse the existing level pegs for this purpose up one side of the ties. The pegs are needed to hold the risers firmly in place. Without the pegs, the ties would only be supported by the hardcore base (except for the first one, where the ground in front of it holds it in place). Drive the pegs in with a sledgehammer to about 4 in. from the top of each riser, and secure them to the face of the sleepers with galvanized nails.

6 Now bring in some hardcore as a base for the treads. The easiest method is probably to wheelbarrow the material in from the top of the steps and tip out the hardcore for

3 After you have dug out all the steps, place the second tie. Use a maul or sledgehammer to drive it down to the peg's level.

4 Use a level to check that the tie is level. Then repeat Steps 3 and 4 with all the other railroad tie risers.

5 Drive a wood peg into both the front corners of the risers in order to give them extra support.

the lowest tread first. Spread out the hardcore with a shovel, and compact it with a tamper to give a firm 2-in. base.

7 After the hardcore has been laid on each tread, cover the wood pegs with soil. The pegs are placed purposefully near the ends of each sleeper to ensure that they are unobtrusive and can easily be covered with soil. Loosen the soil at the sides of the bank, breaking down any steep vertical edges, and allow it to form a gentle slope down to the tread level. In the process, the soil will also tend to obscure the pegs. Add more soil as necessary to form a soft gradient down from the bank. Grass growing on the bank will probably spread to bind the new edges, but you may need to sow grass seed as well. Alternatively, some low ground-cover plants would provide a more decorative edge and integrate the railroad tie steps into the planting scheme of your garden as a whole. This can obviously be done at a later date, at your own convenience.

8 Finally, with all the loose soil cleaned up, lay your chosen surface aggregate on each tread. In this project, slate chips were used. Again, the easiest way to carry this out would be to bring a wheelbarrow filled with stone in from the top of the steps and work your way back up from the first step to the last. Spread out the aggregate with a shovel or a rake, brushing any loose stone off the ties. Gravel will provide a golden, crunchy surface that stands out against the dark ties, while the color of blue-gray slate will harmonize with the greens of the surrounding grass and foliage.

Alternative materials

A loose material such as gravel works especially well in a larger aggregate of, for example, ¾ in. that will not be kicked around so easily. For a more hard-wearing tread, try laying granite setts. Machine-rounded logs, which are smooth, treated timbers with an even diameter that can simply be held in place with pegs, can be used to form the risers as an alternative to railroad ties.

6 Next use a wheelbarrow to tip hardcore onto each step to create a base for each of the treads.

7 Cover up each of the wood corner pegs with soil to disguise them. Then clean up any loose soil that is left.

8 You can now use the wheelbarrow again to place your chosen surface aggregate onto each of the treads.

brick
STEPS

With so many different colors and styles available, and such a variety of patterns possible, brick is an incredibly versatile material. Brick steps provide a strong visual link with the house or with bricks used elsewhere in paving trims or garden walls.

1 Mark out the position of the steps, clearing the topsoil and any vegetation before excavating the shape of the steps. Calculate the number of steps required, the height of the risers, and the depth of the treads. The riser height for bricks should be 7 in., with a tread depth of 13½ in. On one side of the steps, put in a peg at the top and bottom of the bank to indicate the position of the first and last steps. Fix a string line between the tops of these pegs as a reference to show the leading edge of each step.

Most of the weight in a flight of steps will be transferred to the bottom step, so you will need to build the first riser on a concrete footing. To lay this, excavate a trench to about a spade's depth and backfill with a 1:6 concrete mix. Tamp the concrete to produce a smooth, level surface.

2 Make up a 1:6 mortar mix using soft sand, and trowel in a line along the concrete footing (i.e., the full width of the

MATERIALS

Wood pegs

String

Concrete

Mortar

Bricks

Short length of wood for tamping

TOOLS

Groundwork tools

Paving tools

Slab cutter

1 The first riser must be built on a concrete footing. To do this, excavate a trench, place the concrete in, and tamp it down.

2 Lay a mortar mix along the concrete, and then begin to lay your first line of bricks to create the first riser.

KNOW YOUR MATERIALS

Brick makes an ideal material to use for both paving and steps, provided it is suitably frostproof. Some bricks that have a high rate of moisture absorption may be fine in walls where they are protected by a layer of insulation and capping, but will otherwise become saturated in paving and susceptible to freeze and thaw damage.

Bricks may be laid in different patterns and bonds, such as running bond, which laid widthwise will make the steps seem wider, but laid lengthwise will make the steps seem narrower and encourage quicker movement. Stack bond is where bricks are laid to a grid pattern without the joints being staggered at all.

step). Lay a line of bricks onto the bed of mortar to form the first riser, using a set square to ensure that it runs at 90° to the string line.

As you lay the bricks, butter up one end of each brick, then tap it into place. "Buttering" means troweling a wedge of mortar onto the end of the brick that is to be laid against the previous brick, in order to create a mortar-filled joint. When the line of bricks is complete, use a level to check that they are even.

3 Once the first riser has been laid, set in a base of concrete behind the bricks to prepare for the tread. Mix up a 1:6 concrete mix—or possibly slightly weaker—and then shovel it into place to the depth of the riser blocks. You can then smooth it out with a trowel to form a firm, level, solid base for the tread.

4 Next, lay the bricks that will form the tread for the first step on a 1:6 mortar mix (or use a slightly stronger mix for a harder joint). The bricks in this project are laid on

edge and the tread is one-and-a-half bricks deep, so you will need to cut a third of the bricks in half using a bolster or slab cutter.

Starting on the right, lay one full brick at the leading edge of the step, then lay a half-brick behind it. On the left of these, lay one half-brick at the leading edge of the step, then lay a full brick behind it. Continue working from right to left along the step, alternating the full and half-bricks in this way. When you lay the first brick, be sure that it lightly brushes the string line with its front top corner, because this brick will set the level for the whole tread.

5 Once the first tread has been laid, make sure that all the joints within it have been filled with mortar (this includes the riser joints). After you have done this, you can give them a rubbed finish with a short piece of pipe. Any surplus mortar that appears while achieving this rubbed finish can be removed when it is dry by simply brushing it off or by using a trowel to scrape off any of the more stubborn pieces.

3 Place a layer of concrete behind your first riser as a base for the tread, and use a trowel to smooth it out.

4 Take care that the tread's first brick lightly brushes your string line. Then you can place all the rest of the bricks into position.

5 The joints of the tread must be filled with mortar. Once this is done, rub them with a piece of pipe to create a smooth finish.

6 | Now that your first step has been completed, you should shovel in concrete behind its tread to form the base of the next step. Roughly level out this concrete, and then use a trowel as before to create a smooth surface that finishes flush with the top of the brick tread.

7 | You can now trowel mortar in a line across this concrete footing as done previously to create a bed for the second riser. Tap the bricks down into place, ensuring that there is a neat mortar joint showing between the bottom of the brick riser and the brick tread below. If there is not a good joint, not only will the riser be too low, but it will be impossible to create a neat rubbed finish. Therefore, moisture could get under the bricks and cause freeze-thaw damage. Use a level to ensure that the riser bricks are all level and aligned.

8 | Once you have laid all the bricks for the second riser, backfill with concrete behind the riser, leveling up to the top of the brick. Smooth the concrete off, and trowel mortar out for the tread bricks again. Bed the first brick, and gently tap it into place so that it just brushes the string line as before. Continue laying all the tread bricks, repeating the same pattern as used on the first step and pointing up the joints when you have laid them all down. Continue with this process up the bank until the whole flight of steps has been completed. Finally, make sure that all the joints, including the risers, have been properly pointed, and brush off any excess when the mortar is dry.

Alternative ideas

A combination of materials can look superb in steps. For example, bricks, granite, or sandstone setts may be laid as the tread and combined with a riser made from crisp, sawed timber or dressed blocks of stone.

Containers placed on each step, either on one side or at alternate sides, can transform a functional flight of steps into a visual feature. For an even softer look, try planting shrubs and other low plants alongside the steps to grow up and over the edge.

6 You can now place concrete behind the first step's tread, which should be leveled out and smoothed off.

7 The second riser's bricks can now be put into place. These should be tapped down, leaving a neat joint between them and the first tread.

8 As before, lay the first brick of the tread so that it brushes the string. Continue the whole process to lay the remaining steps.

wood DECK STEPS

Wooden deck boards have a smart yet natural appearance and are comfortable enough to double up as warm, relaxed seats. Following a simple box structure, this flight of steps has been designed to run up a short section of bank adjacent to a deck patio.

1 | Calculate the step dimensions so that standard width wood can be used for all risers and treads. Mark out the area, and excavate down to the level of the proposed adjacent deck. Next, dig out holes for the front and back posts of the first step, each to about a spade's width. Set the front posts 9 in. deep and 3 in. above ground level. The back posts will need to be longer, overall about 16 in., in order to form the front posts of the second step. Making sure the 2-in. side of each post faces the front, pour in a 1:6 concrete mix to two-thirds full and firm it around the base of the post. Mark out pencil guidelines on the front posts 3 in. down and 1 in. in from the outside edge. Cut along these lines and remove the wood sections from the outside of the post.

2 | The sections of wood are cut from the front posts in order to form joints for the bearers, so the cuts need to

1 Set the front posts for the first step. Mark on each the dimensions of the bearer and then saw out the wood to leave a joint.

2 Hold the bearer between the front and back posts. Checking that it remains level, mark the joint position on the back post.

KNOW YOUR MATERIALS

These streamlined timber deck steps require no foundations, which makes construction straightforward. Timber may be treated softwood, Western red cedar, or possibly a hardwood such as iroko.

The decking boards may be different widths depending on your design, but try to make steps that fit standard widths of boards, rather than trying to cut the boards down to fit. Wood retailers will be able to advise you on the most

suitable timber to use, and they will also be able to supply grooved timber boards for extra grip. To save on materials, steps can be left open-sided, but to achieve a neat and sturdy appearance, it is best to box in the edges.

be straight so the bearers fit flush. Wood bearers are placed along the side of each step to connect the posts of one step to the next and to support the deck treads. To get the bearers straight, place one in the joint of the first post and extend it back to the second post. Place a level on the bearer and mark the second post with a pencil along the top and bottom edge of the bearer to show the joint's position. Do this on both sides of the front step.

3 Make the joints for the bearers of the second step on the second posts. The bottom of the new joint should be 1 in. up from the top of the lower joint, and it should extend upward for 3 in. Cut the new joint and trim the top of the post to the height of the joint.

For the lower joints, make two horizontal saw cuts along the pencil guidelines marked out in Step 2 until you have cut halfway through the posts.

4 Start to remove the wood from the lower joint by chiseling in from each side. Try not to take out too much wood at once, and when it has all been removed, use sandpaper to get rid of any splinters so that you end up with a smooth joint to allow the bearers to fit flush.

5 You can now tap both bearers into place for the bottom step. Nail the bearers into place using two galvanized nails at each joint. Continue this process for the whole flight of steps, notching joints in all the posts and fixing bearers in place. For additional stability, fix another beam between the two back posts of the top step, notching joints a couple of inches below the last bearers into the back face of each post. Once all the bearers have been nailed in, top up the post holes with concrete to just above ground level. Check that the posts are all upright with a level before finally firming the concrete around them. Leave the concrete to harden overnight.

6 You can now start adding deck boards to the step framework. Nail on the first deck board so that it sits over the front posts, having first cut it to size. Make sure the

3 Having cut the top joint, make two horizontal cuts halfway through the second post along the guidelines marked out for the bottom joint.

4 After the horizontal cuts have been made, chisel in from each side to remove the wood from the lower joint section.

5 The bearers can now be slotted into the spaces you have made and should be fixed securely with galvanized nails.

leading edge of this board sits flush with the front edge of the posts. Cut all the deck boards to length and set them out on the first tread using a pencil as a spacer between them. Set them out until they sit evenly between the first board already in place and the front of the second posts. Tap a nail through the end of each board into the bearer, but do not drive it all the way in. This will ensure that you are still able to lift and reposition the boards if the spacing goes awry. When you are satisfied that all the tread boards are in their correct positions, double-nail both ends of each board. Continue to nail deck boards in this way until all the step treads are completed.

7 | Now, attach fascia boards to the front of each step to form the risers. Using wood that is of the same dimensions as the deck boards, cut the fascia boards to length and nail them to the front of each step with two nails at each end of the boards. Position each fascia board so that it rests flush on the last board of each tread, with its top edge finishing flush with the tread of the next step.

8 | Using fascia boards of the same dimensions, box in the step sides to conceal the ends of the deck board, giving a neat and professional finish to the steps. Try to plan it so that the board at the side of the first step extends past the side of the second step, and so on, up the entire flight of steps, since this will look neater than having a joint at the side of each riser.

In this project, the top step has been extended to twice its width to form an open-fronted seat that is easily constructed. Set in a front and back post to the left-hand side of the seat. As this is an open-fronted seat, the posts will be seen and should look sturdy, so you should use 3 × 3 in. posts. Set them in concrete so that their finished height allows for a deck board to be nailed over the top. Cut joints into the left-hand edges of the post tops to hold a bearer. Nail the bearer into position and then attach extra-long deck boards that extend across from the top step to form the seat. Complete by nailing 1 × 2 in. fascia boards to the front and side of the seat to box in the deck boards.

6 Now start laying deck boards to form the treads. Place a pencil between each board to ensure that spacing is equal throughout.

7 Once the treads are all in place, measure and cut fascia boards and nail them to the front of each step to create the risers.

8 Box in the sides of the steps to conceal the ends of the boards. Try to avoid forming joints at the side of each riser.

natural STONE STEPS

You don't need to own a stately home to choose natural stone steps for your garden. They look just as impressive in the backyard of an urban town house, and they also fit in perfectly with the rural charm of a country garden.

1 | Calculate the number of steps, depth of tread, and height of riser for the first flight up to the landing and from this point up to the top. The upper flight is laid at 90° to the lower flight. Mark out the position of the steps, clear the ground, and roughly excavate the step shapes in the bank.

Working from the bottom, fix wood pegs along the side of the steps to indicate the finished height of each step. Fix the first peg at the correct height for the first step. Knock in the second peg to roughly the right height, and then lay a level across from the top of the first peg to the second. Measure up from the underside of the level to the desired height of the second step, and tap the second peg down to exactly the right level. Continue in this way, positioning marker pegs for each step up to the landing.

2 | For strength, lay the riser of the bottom step on a concrete footing. Excavate a trench to about a spade's depth and

MATERIALS

Wood pegs

Concrete

Mortar

Walling stone blocks

Riven stone paving

TOOLS

Groundwork tools

Paving tools

1 Measure up from the bottom of a level, laid from the top of the first peg back to the second, to gain the height of the second riser.

2 Having first laid concrete footings, place walling blocks on a mortar base to form the first riser and returns.

KNOW YOUR MATERIALS

The hard-wearing properties and frost-proof surface of sandstone paving make it the best material for the treads in a flight of stone steps. Sandstone is usually supplied in random rectangular flagstones that have been split out from large quarried blocks of stone. This type of flagstone has a "riven face," which means it may be slightly uneven on the surface. A sandstone with a smoother finish—diamond-sawed paving—is available. It is more expensive but looks very sharp. A textured surface can be given to this type of stone for extra grip. Sandstone may also be used for the walling blocks that form the risers and returns, normally 4 in. wide in random lengths.

width before filling in with a 1:6 concrete mix. Spread a 1:6 mortar mix along the footing. The mortar can be made either with sharp or soft sand, but sharp sand may give a firmer bed for heavy stone blocks. Select walling blocks to show a good face at the front of the riser. Butter the ends of the blocks with mortar, and tap them down into position. Lay more stone blocks to form the returns of the steps at 90° to the riser. Again, excavate a trench and fill it with concrete, then bed down the blocks on a mortar base, filling the joints with mortar as you go.

3 When the riser and returns for the first step are complete, backfill behind them with a 1:6 concrete mix, and trowel out the concrete to finish level with the top of the blocks. Again, spread mortar of the same 1:6 mix used for the risers over the concrete base. Choose flagstones with good, square corners, and lay them down on the mortar bed so that they overhang the stonework by no more than 2 in. Tap these slabs down with a club hammer handle or maul, laying a level across to the wood peg

every so often to check for the correct height. Lay the paving with a very slight fall toward the front so that it will shed any surface water.

4 Having completed the first step, backfill behind it with a shovelful of concrete to form a level base upon which to bed the second riser. Lay the riser blocks on a mortar bed, filling up the joints with mortar as well. You may have to lay some stone blocks underneath the side returns to get the desired height, depending on the gradient of the bank.

5 Backfill concrete behind the riser blocks, smoothing it out to form a firm base upon which to lay the next tread. Each flight can be formed from however many steps you would like or require, but for this project, the second step forms the landing and is paved with larger flagstones accordingly. These larger flagstones will probably require two people to lift them into place.

Try to plan the paving of the treads so that the joints are staggered from one step to the next as you progress up

3 As you lay flagstones for the first step, place a level across to the wood peg now and again to check for the correct height.

4 The next riser can be built now, although you may need to lay some stone blocks underneath the side to ensure that the height is correct.

5 Each of the paving treads should overhang its riser by about 2 in. to hide the mortar joints beneath.

the steps, and make sure that the tread overhangs the riser by approximately 2 in. This is so that it will form a shadow line that will hide the mortar joint.

6 The flight of steps that leads up from the landing should be at 90° to the first flight. To get this angle correct, ensure that the second flight starts parallel with the far edge of the landing slabs by measuring the width of the landing in two places. The two measurements to the front of the next riser should be equal to ensure that this step is at right angles to the first flight. Check that the positioning of the next riser looks right by placing some stone blocks in position temporarily, then bed them down when satisfied.

7 In this project, the second flight of steps has been designed so that it is narrower than the width of the landing. Therefore, it will be partially laid on the flagstones. Again, spread out a mortar bed and tap the stone riser blocks into position, ensuring that all joints are properly filled and that the blocks are correctly aligned.

8 Backfill with concrete behind the riser, smoothing off to a level finish before spreading out a bed of mortar for the next tread. The corner of this tread can be seen clearly, so be sure to choose a flagstone with a good corner. Continue to lay the remaining steps using the same method as before. When finished, point up the joints with either the same mortar mix or a stronger 1:4 mix, and leave them with a rubbed finish. Clean off any surplus mortar when dry. The steps are now finished, and you can plant up around them, place pots on the landing, or position pots on each step.

Alternative materials

In this project, we have used sandstone, but limestone is one possible alternative as a material for the risers. However, it is not suitable for paving the treads, as its surface may be damaged in frosty conditions. Slate, which ranges in color from green to dark blue to black, can be cut in random pieces to form smart step treads with risers in slate blocks or thin pieces of horizontally bedded slate.

6 Once the landing has been built, you will need to measure across it to determine where to put your next step.

7 When building this next riser, which will be partially on the landing, you will still need to be sure that the joints of the walling blocks are filled.

8 As this step is the first you see when turning the corner on the landing, make sure you choose the best possible flagstone.

patios

planning for patios

More than just a drab area of concrete outside the back door, patios have become the focus of family life in the garden. Stone terraces and streamlined wood decks are perfect for a lunchtime barbecue and candlelit dinner parties, while areas of textured paving form the ideal nonslip surface for children's play. A small, secluded brick patio surrounded by perfumed shrubs may be the perfect place for a relaxing drink or a snooze on a comfortable bench.

Function and style A patio is a paved area of the garden that is normally located next to the house and forms the center of outdoor family life, both in terms of entertaining and relaxation. It helps to prevent mud from being carried indoors and offers a convenient location for eating outside. Sometimes the best position for a patio is a sunny location farther out in the garden, from where views can be enjoyed back over the garden toward the house. It is therefore essential that patios look right with the house and their location within the garden. A broad stone terrace close to the house allows space for dining outside, while a smaller paved area away from the house works well with materials such as brick or setts, as their small unit size is perfect for creating a more intimate and compact circular patio. Plants will help to soften the lines of paving and will also ensure that a patio feels comfortably enclosed and sheltered from the elements.

Design choices Patios must be in proportion to the scale of the house and garden. Avoid low perimeter walls along the edge of ground-level patios, as they are a nuisance for maintenance and serve no purpose other than to cut the patio off from the rest of the garden. Areas of paving set into a bank, however, will need retaining walls around the edge. A raised patio or terrace can be really effective for sitting outside overlooking the garden when the ground slopes away from the rear of the house. Timber decks work particularly well in this situation, and this type of construction also avoids expensive foundations and retaining walls. Simple designs usually look best. Instead of cutting slabs to a curved edge, for example, a cleaner effect can be achieved by staggering the edge slabs and planting against them to

Decking interspersed with loose aggregate.

Geometric slab and sett design.

Colored mosaic cobblestones.

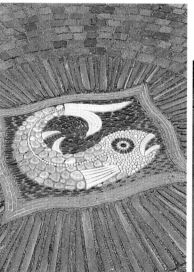

Colored tiles and gray slabs.

The design style of your patio is a key consideration when planning your garden layout. The brick and slab squares (top left) provide an interesting contrast in texture and color. The timber decking patio (top right) is perfectly set off with matching deck steps—these can provide a link from the patio to other parts of the garden, for example, the pebble path seen here. The geometric lines of the mosaic patio (above) are softened by the natural style of the flowering shrubs planted around the edges.

Irregularly shaped stone slabs, laid in a random pattern and surrounded by lush planting.

create a soft, curved line. Flagstones and good imitations in precast concrete work well when laid in a random pattern. Slabs laid in a running-bond pattern or staggered joint introduce visual movement through the space, while paving laid in a grid pattern is more static, looking good in a courtyard and especially in a contemporary design.

Plants are a crucial part of patio design, linking the area with the garden and creating soft foundation plants to break the hard line against the house or perimeter wall. Fragrant shrubs and herbs work well.

Types of paving A huge range of materials can be used to surface patios, including natural stone and many good imitations. These always work well with a brick trim and insets to form a visual link with a brick house. Natural stone is best laid in a sunny location to keep the surface from becoming too slippery. It usually has a riven surface, which can make it too uneven for small children to run around on without tripping. Natural stone can be supplied as sawed paving that has a more even surface, and it can also be given a gritty, textured surface for better grip.

> *Combinations of different materials often work well for patios, particularly brick and stone paving.*

Precast concrete slabs are also available with a textured surface, which is useful not only for areas of dappled shade, but also in children's gardens where an even, nonslip patio is required. Small paving units such as bricks are fine for a courtyard or small sitting area but would look too busy in a large patio. If you decide to use bricks, then the clay ones work much better than the concrete kind. Natural stone setts are also available; sandstone is more even than granite, although it is slippery in the shade. There are some excellent imitations, however, in precast concrete. Imitation terra-cotta tiles link well with interior floors surfaced in the same material, and when surrounded with plants in pots, evoke a Mediterranean atmosphere. Decking in a sunny location looks superb, but only when set against the right property; it may be out of place against a period home where natural stone would be more appropriate.

Combinations of different materials often work well, particularly brick and stone paving. Loose pebbles set at the base of plants around a patio create a good transition from the hard paved surface to the surrounding soft landscape. Small mosaics look wonderful set into areas of paving, as do the sparkling points of light when small pieces of colored glass are set into joints around darker paving.

You may choose to use one single type of material when constructing your patio. Brick, when used on its own, for example, is particularly well suited for creating crisp geometric patterns (above right). You can also combine two or more types of materials. The timber decking patio (above left), for example, is complemented by a raised platform, which is made out of large, light-gray concrete slabs interspersed with small, dark-gray bricks.

Multicolored tiles.

Slate in an informal pattern.

Gray stone slabs with grass and water.

Granite setts.

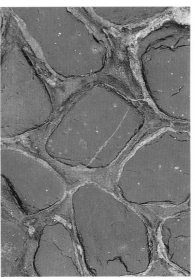

textured
SLAB PATIO

A patio laid with textured paving is ideal for a family garden if you have young children. It is also useful for other areas where a nonslip surface is required, such as around a swimming pool or in the shade of overhanging trees where moss may grow.

1 | Mark around and excavate the patio area, allowing for a 3-in. depth of hardcore and 3 in. for the combined depth of the mortar bed and slabs. Textured paving can be laid directly onto a screeded bed of mortar covering the entire area to be paved, rather than placing the mortar in ridges and furrows under each slab.

After compacting a layer of hardcore, lay out screed rails across the hardcore base at about 5-ft. intervals, depending on the overall size of the patio. The rails are lengths of wood of a thickness equal to the depth of the mortar bed, approximately 1½ in. There is no need to fix the rails, as their function is simply to support wood that is used for the screeding process.

2 | Make up a mix of fairly dry 1:6 mortar, and tip it out onto the hardcore. Use a shovel to push the mortar around to a rough level before screeding. With a straight piece of

MATERIALS

Hardcore

Pegs

String

Wood screed rails

Wood straightedge

Mortar

Textured slabs

Kiln-dried sand

TOOLS

Groundwork tools

Paving tools

1 Having excavated and laid the hardcore base across the area that will form your patio, position screed rails across it at 5-ft. intervals.

2 Put a layer of mortar on top of the hardcore and use a piece of wood positioned on the rails to screed it out flush with the screed rails.

KNOW YOUR MATERIALS

Textured paving normally comes in the form of precast concrete slabs. The slabs are produced in a range of different textures, sizes, and colors, so they are ideal for all types of setting, both traditional and modern. Use them to form random paving patterns, or if only a couple of sizes are used, then a more streamlined design can be created. Although slabs are produced in several colors, natural-colored (which are almost white) and buff-colored slabs give the most satisfactory results. As the slabs do not have a riven surface to imitate traditional natural stone, they look good when used in crisp, contemporary designs.

wood laid across from one screed rail to the other, screed the mortar to the correct level.

Keep screeding the mortar until it is all flush with the tops of the rails. However, it is a good idea to screed out only as much mortar as you think you will be able to pave over within an hour, or it will be wasted because it will dry out and become unusable.

3 Once you have finished screeding, carefully remove the rails without disturbing the mortar and fill in the resulting gaps. You can do this by troweling mortar into these gaps and then smoothing it off with the back of the trowel. Alternatively, rather than smooth with the trowel, you can gently run a straightedge of wood once more across the mortar to smooth off the filled-in gaps.

4 Set up string lines around the edges of the patio to show the finished height of paving. Do this by setting up pegs in the four corners and running the string lines around them.

You can now begin to lay the slabs. It is important to spend time getting the first slab correctly positioned, since it will set the slope for the others. Lay the slab in one of the corners so that it lightly touches the two string lines marking the edges, and very gently tap it into position.

5 Continue to lay the slabs in the same manner, building up your pattern as you go. Jointing patterns can be truly random, with different slab sizes laid with no attempt made at an obvious pattern. Some manufacturers print out examples of random patterns for different widths of patios, which is useful when ordering the right quantity of slabs for each size.

If you do not want to use a pattern at all, then it is best to let the supplier know the size of the area you are planning to pave. They should be able to advise you on the correct quantity of each slab size so that you are not left with too many big or small slabs that cannot be worked into the pattern. Whether or not you lay to a pattern, the most important thing to remember about

3 Once you have removed the rails, fill the gaps that appear with mortar, smoothing them off with a trowel.

4 Set up string lines to indicate the finished height of the patio, and then you can lay the first slab using the strings as a guide.

5 Lay all the slabs in a random style, incorporating the occasional small slab and placing others around it.

random-style paving is that you should avoid long joints. To do this, try to lay occasional small squares around which the other slabs radiate.

6 Textured paving slabs have crisp, even edges, allowing them to butt up tightly against each other. The slabs can be laid with mortar joints, but they are manufactured to be laid butt-jointed, which gives a smarter appearance overall. When butt-jointing slabs, it is important to scrape away any particles of mortar from the slab edge so that the next slab fits tightly against it. If the slabs do not butt together well, there is a danger that the joints will begin to loosen, and this will make laying subsequent slabs much harder.

7 When all the slabs have been laid, smooth off the mortar around the edge of the patio with a trowel. The next day, after the slabs have set firm, you will be able to walk on them in order to spread fine, kiln-dried sand across the patio, brushing it in with a soft brush to seal the joints.

After a few days, the sand will combine with general dirt to form a tight seal, binding all the slabs together.

Alternative methods

Since textured slabs do not imitate natural stone, they are ideally suited to gardens with a more contemporary feel. If you are aiming for a more uniform appearance than the random pattern described here, paving units in rectangles can be laid for pathways in 90° herringbone or running bond (see below). Both of these patterns will also lend a strong sense of movement to the patio. If you wish to create a geometric courtyard design, square slabs are more suitable.

Alternative materials

Many well-fired bricks have a sandy texture on their faces, making them useful for small patios and courtyards. Natural stone can also be bought with a textured finish for extra grip, and sandstone, one of the best natural materials for paving, is also available with a gritty finish.

6 You must make sure that you scrape away any mortar that appears at the edges of the slabs, so they can be butt-jointed neatly.

7 When you have finished laying the slabs, spread kiln-dried sand across them all, brushing it into the joints to seal them.

Alternative method: A more uniform patio can be created using rectangular paving laid in a running bond.

circular PATIO

If you are yearning for a private space in your garden to make the most of a sunny spot, a small circular patio is perfect for creating a sense of intimacy. With patio kits available that contain all you need to lay a complicated circular design without cutting any slabs, it could not be easier.

1 Decide where in your garden you want to position your patio, and then using the triangulation method set out on page 18, fix the center point of the circle in the lawn to mark the middle of the patio. Drive in a steel pin or wood peg at this point and tie a string line to it. Then attach a screwdriver or nail to a string that is the exact length of the circle's radius and pull the line taut.

Now walk around the circumference of the circle, scoring a mark on the turf to indicate the outside edge of the patio. Make the scraped line in the turf more visible by sprinkling sand along it or by marking it with spray paint.

2 Start excavation by digging around the edge line, then work toward the center from opposite points. This will ensure an even depth of excavation and avoid overdigging. If you start excavating at one side of the patio and work your way across it, there is a danger that your excavations

MATERIALS

String

Steel pin or wood peg

Hardcore

Mortar

Circular paving kit

Wood straightedge

Clay bricks (if desired)

Gravel

TOOLS

Groundwork tools

Paving tools

Plate compactor

1 Once you have measured out and scored the circumference of the circle on the turf, sprinkle sand on the outline to make it more visible.

2 Begin your excavation of the area by digging up around the perimeter. Be sure you allow for the layer of hardcore and mortar.

KNOW YOUR MATERIALS

Many paving suppliers now produce a variety of patio kits with imitation riven natural stone slabs that can be laid on their own or can form an interesting link with larger patios of the same material.

Many different patterns are available, but usually the circular or hexagonal patios provide the best results. Most types of precast concrete slabs can now be obtained in units to make up a circular patio. The radial-shaped pieces in

different dimensions can be laid to form one-, two-, or three-ring circles, depending on the size of the patio. A good way to make the concrete appear more natural is to fill the joints with gravel rather than mortar, as shown here.

will get deeper and deeper. When digging, allow for the thickness of the slab plus a 1½-in. depth of mortar and a 3-in. depth of hardcore.

3 Having finished the excavation, drive in four pegs just outside the circumference to indicate the finished height of the patio. Site the pegs at each end of two diameter lines that dissect the patio area into four equal quarters. Attach string lines over the tops of opposite pairs of pegs so that the lines cross over the center point. These will provide a reference point to check for the correct depth of hardcore and to indicate the finished paving height. Make sure the string lines are set up accurately to show the alignment of the patio. This might mean that one of the lines runs parallel to the back of the house if that is how the patio has been planned. The other line should be set at 90° to the first one using a 3:4:5 triangle.

You can then shovel in the hardcore and compact it down using a plate compactor to give a sufficient clearance under the string lines for the paving and mortar.

4 Once a level base has been created, you can prepare for the laying of the paving, which should always be started from the center and never the outside. If you start laying slabs from the outside, there is the possibility that the inside slabs will not quite fit. The slabs will need to be laid onto mortar, so spread a few shovels of 1:6 mortar mix on top of the compacted hardcore. Then lay two of the center quadrants side by side, with both their straight edges touching the string lines that you set up. You should tap them down until they sit flush with the string lines.

Then lay the first band of surrounding segment slabs, putting down mortar for each slab as you work your way around. Use the string lines as a guide for both the positioning and the finished height.

5 If your kit has more bands, you can go on to lay the second band of segment slabs in exactly the same way, using the first band as a guide for positioning. Each patio slab should be tapped into place leaving an open joint for pointing. It is often a good idea to lay the circle out dry to

3 Set up pegs and string lines to indicate the center of the patio and its finished height, then lay hardcore and compact it down.

4 Start by laying the first two center quadrants, making sure that their straight edges touch the string lines. Then lay the surrounding slabs.

5 The second band of slabs can be laid down next if there is one, leaving a joint between each to be pointed up later.

one side of the area, just to check how it all fits together. This will also ensure that you always pick up the correct piece to lay, because you can just take the next one along.

6 Once you have laid the first few bands, place a wood straightedge across the slabs as work progresses to ensure that all the pieces fit flush with each other. Continue to lay the segments to complete one half of the circle first, as you will find this easier than trying to work around the whole circle all at once.

7 Lay the second half of the circle, then if desired, lay down an edging of bricks. We have chosen to use clay bricks here, which take a long time to lay but have an attractive appearance. You will need to lay the clay bricks on a bed of mortar once again. Follow the curve of the paving around, keeping the joint between the bricks adjacent to the paving as tight as possible, so that the outer joint is not too wide. Pack the outside of the bricks with mortar when they are all laid.

8 Once all the paving units are in place, brush gravel into the joints of the whole patio. This produces a softer appearance than mortar-pointed joints.

Spread the gravel with a shovel and use a soft broom to brush the material into the joints, leaving the joints slightly recessed so that the gravel is not kicked around when it is walked on. Sweep up any excess. You can now either lay new turf around the edge of the patio or grow plants in the area, as desired.

Alternative materials

Imitation brick or tile edges of about 24 in. long are also produced for creating a trim to the paving slabs. They are certainly quick and easy to lay, but some varieties can look like obvious imitations. However, there are plenty of better-quality bricks available.

Mortar can be used to point up all the joints in the slabs, rather than the gravel. The best mix for this is 1:4 mortar. However, if you would like moss to grow through and soften the joints, a weaker mix could be used.

6 Place a straightedge of wood over the slabs you have laid to make sure that they are all flush with one another.

7 Once all the slabs have been laid, you could lay an edging of bricks around them. Bed the bricks into a layer of mortar.

8 After the patio is completely laid, spread gravel into all the joints, and use a soft broom to brush it into place.

stone and
BRICK PATIO

Sandstone is probably the best natural stone to use for patio paving. Its golden color mellows with age, weathering beautifully and providing a real sense of permanence.

1 | Mark out the patio and then set a datum peg to one side of this area. The patio should be level from side to side and incorporate a slope of 1:60 from back to front. Decide on the finished level of the patio along its back edge, and using a level and tape measure, check the measurement down to this finished level from the top of the datum.

Next determine the finished level of the front edge, applying the slope, and check this measurement down from the top of the datum. The overall depth of excavation will be 7 in., which is the sum of the paving thickness of 2½ in., mortar depth of 1½ in., and the foundation of 3 in., allowing slightly more at the front of the patio for the slope.

2 | With a strong spade, dig out a trench along the back, followed by one along the front of the patio area. Once

MATERIALS

Hardcore

Sharp sand

Soft sand

Cement

Random rectangular sandstone paving (1 ton/20 cwt of 2½-in. slabs for 7 sq. yd.)

Wood straightedge

Selection of paving bricks

TOOLS

Groundwork tools

Paving tools

Stone cutter

Plate compactor

Concrete mixer

1 Set up a datum peg to one side of the area, against which all levels will be determined using a level and tape measure.

2 After excavating the patio, apply a layer of hardcore and compact it down to a depth of 3 in. with a plate compactor.

KNOW YOUR MATERIALS

Natural sandstone lends warmth to any outdoor area, and it blends well with other materials and plants. Here, paving bricks add interest between the slabs and provide a subtle contrast of color and texture. Hard, egg-shaped, beach cobblestones would work equally well. The riven, textured surface of the sandstone is produced by splitting the rock along its natural bed face, which is best for paving. Not only does this give sandstone a naturally ornamental finish, but it also makes the patio surface less likely to become slippery in wet weather. The slabs are supplied by weight in random rectangular sizes with their rough edges trimmed or fettled.

these two trenches are at the right depth, the area between them can be dug out to complete the excavation. As work progresses, check the depth by measuring down from a level held across the top of the datum peg. The correct depth is the distance from the top of the datum to the finished level of the patio plus 7 in. Excavate an area slightly wider than the patio so that there is a sufficient base width of hardcore and to make it easier for you to lay the edge slabs.

Spread hardcore over the area to a depth of 3½ in. and compact it down to 3 in. with a plate compactor. Measure down from the datum peg to check that the foundation is at the correct level of 4 in. down from finished paving level. Add more hardcore to any low spots, as this is cheaper than filling with mortar.

3 Set up two string lines at right angles to each other to mark the back edge and one side of the patio. Indicate the finished level of the paving along these edges. Take your time setting these lines out accurately, as they set the finished height and slope on the first few slabs from which the others follow.

4 Make a 1:6 mortar mix on which to bed the flagstones (although a weaker mix may be adequate). Start in the corner where the string lines meet and spread a few shovelfuls of mortar over the hardcore. The mix should be a little firmer than that used for other paving in order to support these heavy flagstones. Use a trowel to create a series of ridges and furrows in the mortar screed so that the slab can be tapped down into place. Make sure that you have laid enough mortar so that when the slabs are initially placed on top, they sit about ¼ in. higher than the finished level.

5 Select a good-sized stone slab with two edges forming a right angle for a cornerstone. Lay it gently, wriggling it down into the mortar bed. Push the slab down so that it sits just above the string lines. Next gently tap it into place with a rubber maul until both edges are flush with the

3 Set up two string lines to indicate the finished paving level, the line of the back edge, and one side of the patio.

4 Use a trowel to make ridges and furrows in the mortar bed so that the slab can be tapped down to the right level.

5 Start with a cornerstone and position it gently into the mortar bed, pushing it down until it sits just above the string line.

lines along the top. Get help to lift the heavy slab, if necessary. Lay slabs on either side of this cornerstone using the string lines and the first slab as a guide. Continue to pave the patio area, building up a random pattern and avoiding long, straight joints. Create an even blend of sizes within the pattern, avoiding any large groups of small pieces. To form gaps into which the bricks and cobblestones can be inserted, simply leave out some of the smaller pieces, but make sure you clean out the mortar in these gaps promptly, before it sets.

6 Lay a brick or slab at the finished level of the bottom edge of the patio to act as a temporary guide. Then place a wood straightedge measuring 2 in. × 3 in. × 10 ft. across from the top to the bottom edges of the patio to ensure that the tops of all the slabs finish flush with the underside of the wood. Tap down any uneven slabs with a maul, as needed. Leave joints of about ⅜ in. between each slab, and scrape out any mortar in the joint before it hardens. Finish laying all the slabs, cutting any as necessary, or leaving a

toothed edge against planting areas. Cover and leave to dry overnight.

7 The next day, you can start to lay bricks in the gaps between the stones. First, scrape out some of the hardcore, and then lay a bed of the same mortar mix. Lay the bricks either flat or on edge. Tap down bricks to finish flush with the surrounding paving using a block of wood and a club hammer. If you are laying cobblestones instead, set them in mortar to about two-thirds of their depth to make sure that they remain firm, and tap them down to finish flush with the paving.

8 Choose a dry day for pointing the joints to avoid smearing mortar over the slabs. Mix a crumbly 1:4 mortar (one part cement, two parts sharp sand, two parts soft sand). Pack it into the joints with a trowel so it is flush with the paving. Then use a short section of pipe to produce a rubbed finish. Scrape off excess mortar the following day and brush the paving, prior to rinsing it off.

6 Use a rubber maul to tap the slabs down into place. Lay a wood straightedge across the patio to get the level of each stone right.

7 Use a block of wood and a club hammer to tap the bricks down so that they finish flush with the paving stones.

8 Use a crumbly mortar to point the joints between the bricks. Make sure that it finishes flush with the tops of the bricks.

cobblestone PATIO

Laying cobblestones to form intricate patterns is one of the oldest and most beautiful types of paving. Such patterns are stunning on a huge scale, but they work equally well for a small, intimate patio, creating an atmospheric seating area.

1 Mark out your proposed seating area, excavating down to allow for 4 in. of hardcore, a 1½-in. depth of mortar, and the depth of pebbles, which is likely to be about 2–3 in. Spread and compact down the hardcore, building in a slope of about 1:40 toward the flower bed or lawn to shed surface water. Fix a temporary edging using 1 × 3 in. boards attached to wood pegs, so that the top of the edging lies at what will be the finished height of the paving. This temporary edging will support the cobblestones as they set.

Screed a thin covering of mortar over the hardcore, as it is necessary to have an even surface to work on. Then set in a second edging board, using a level to make sure it is level with the first, to frame the border pattern.

2 Make up a fairly stiff 1:6 mortar mix and trowel it in between the edgings. Place the cobblestones on end and

MATERIALS

Hardcore

Mortar

Edging boards 1 × 3 in.

Pegs

Black and white cobblestones

TOOLS

Groundwork tools

Paving tools

Board for tapping down stones

Soft brush

Watering can with nozzle attachment

1 Put the two edging boards in position, using a level to ensure that they are both at the same height.

2 Once a layer of mortar has been put between the boards, put the cobblestones on their ends and push them into it.

KNOW YOUR MATERIALS

Cobblestones are small, rounded stones that may be beach pebbles or stones from areas of ancient glacial activity, rounded by the ice. Reject stones from gravel pits are also available as egg-shaped pebbles. These range in size from 1 to 3 in. Cobblestones are available in many different colors, such as the blue, gray, and white varieties that are used in this project. However, you can also get greens and browns for a more earthy feel. The small size of cobblestones makes them perfect for experimenting with more artistic garden surface design. Combined with ceramics and pieces of glass, they can be used to create wonderful mosaic-style patterns.

push them down into the mortar. Be careful to keep the stones as close together as possible and lay them in orderly rows so that the overall pattern can be created.

3 After a short area has been filled with cobblestones, tap them down with a club hammer over a piece of wood so that the tops of the stones finish flush with the tops of the edgings. Continue working in this way around the entire border, pushing stones into the mortar and then tapping them to the correct height as you go.

4 Change the direction in which you place the cobblestones when you reach the corner of the patio, so that the lines of cobblestones continue to run parallel. You will need to place more wood edging down to guide you as you did before. You can now actually remove the edging from the first section so that you can pack mortar up against the cobblestones to hold them firmly in place. It is often best, however, to leave the outer edge until the end of the job, so that it can hold everything in place to set.

5 This project follows a similar patio design to the finished picture shown on the previous page, except that the diamond shapes are set against the edge of the patio to create smaller triangles. To lay the diamond pattern, you will need to construct wood frames approximately 18 in. square, from 1 x 3 in. wood, and set them into position by measuring in from the corners of the border pattern to make sure that the diamond shape is straight. (In order to ensure that the patio is full of complete, rather than half, diamonds, you need to measure carefully before constructing the wood frames, as they may need to be slightly larger or smaller than the measurements given to fit your patio size.) The pattern of cobblestones in the diamond needs to touch the inside of the border. In order for this to work, the frame must be set just into the border pattern. To achieve this, remove a laid cobblestone from the border pattern at both points where the corners of the diamond pattern will meet.

Lay a bed of mortar in the space to bring it level with the outside edge of the patio. Put the corners of it into

3 Tap the pebbles with a club hammer positioned on a piece of wood until they are at the same height as the edging.

4 Having laid your second strip of cobblestones using the same method as before, go back to pack mortar up against the first.

5 Create a wood frame that you can then use as a guide to show you where your diamond pattern should be laid.

the spaces you created in the border in order to prevent any gaps from being left between the diamond and the border pattern. The cobblestones should be replaced when you are finished.

6 Make sure that you use a straightedge or level to check that the frame sits at the correct height before laying any of the cobblestones. You can then place the stones into the frame starting with dark cobblestones, by pushing them into mortar and gently tapping them down using the same method that you did for the border.

7 When the first diamond of dark cobblestones has been laid, set into place the triangles of white cobblestones on either side of it. To do this, first remove the wood frame and pack mortar tightly around the dark cobblestones to hold them in place. Position a board to run along the side of the diamond shape, meeting the inside of the border. This board will act as a temporary edge restraint while laying the cobblestones and will show you where to place

them. Trowel mortar behind the board and push the white cobblestones into place to form the triangular shapes. Continue laying this pattern of diamonds and triangles until the whole terrace is complete.

8 When all the cobblestones have been laid, make up a strong 1:4 dry mix of mortar and spread it over the surface of the stones with a shovel. Use a soft brush to work the mortar between stones, ensuring that none is left on the surface of the cobblestones. Then, use a watering can with a nozzle attachment to water in the dry mix, which will set to hold the stones firmly in position. You will then be able to remove any remaining edging boards before preparing the surrounding area for planting.

Alternative uses

The same method that is shown here for fixing cobblestones into a mortar bed to create a patio can also be used for a decorative pathway, or just as a neat little detail to prevent corners from being cut across a lawn.

6 Once the frame has been set in place, use a level to ensure that it is at the right height before you start laying the cobblestones.

7 Set up a wood board as an edging for the triangle of white pebbles that will surround the dark diamond you have just laid.

8 Once your patio is completely laid, spread a mortar mix over it to hold the cobblestones firmly in position.

decking PATIO

Decking creates an instant tropical feel and is indispensable on warm, sunny days. This patio is attached to the house, providing easy access to a platform from which to view the surrounding garden.

MATERIALS

Treated softwood or Western red cedar

Wood beams 2 x 6 in.

Wood posts 3 x 4 in. or 4 x 4 in.

Wood joists and fascia boards 2 x 4 in.

Wood deck boards available in widths of 4 or 6 in. and in thicknesses of 1 or 1½ in.

Wall plugs and rustproof screws

Galvanized nails

Deck or stainless-steel screws

Gravel

Concrete

Wood stain

TOOLS

Groundwork tools

Woodwork tools

Level

Circular saw

Paintbrush

1 | The best way to fix a deck against a house is to screw a timber beam, or batten, onto the wall—this will give a solid, level base upon which to fix the deck joists. The piece of batten should measure 2 x 6 in., which will be the same dimensions as the beams. The position for the batten can be calculated by measuring down from what will be the finished level of the deck, taking into account the thickness of the deck boards and the joists. Hold the batten level against the wall and drill through to mark the hole positions on the wall. If possible, try to plan it so that the holes will be in a mortar joint, as this will make drilling easier. Set in wall plugs and attach the batten to the wall using long screws.

2 | Before starting work on the rest of the decking frame, it is a good idea to clear and roughly level the area to be covered with decking before covering it with gravel.

2 You will now need to measure out where your supporting posts should be. It is often best to set them at 5-ft. intervals.

1 To fix the decking to your house, attach a wood beam to the wall next to which the deck will be located.

KNOW YOUR MATERIALS

Decking slats may be smooth or grooved to provide extra grip, and the timber can be chosen from many different woods. Pressure-treated softwood, usually pine, is relatively cheap and can be stained easily.

However, check the wood before buying, because very cheap softwood can be full of knots and have poor structural strength. Hardwoods, such as iroko, are incredibly strong, but they are very expensive and difficult to work with.

Even though it is a softwood, Western red cedar is often the best decking timber because of its tight grain, built-in resin (which acts as a preservative), and coloring, which weathers to a beautiful silver.

This will provide a clean surface to work on, and the gravel will also help to prevent weeds from growing up from underneath the deck, where they will be particularly difficult to access.

Having prepared the gravel, measure out from the house to fix the positions for the supporting posts. Depending on the length of the deck, you may need two, three, or even more posts positioned at approximately 5-ft. intervals along the front of the deck, parallel with the house. The posts should have dimensions of 3 × 4 in. or 4 × 4 in.

3 Dig holes for the posts at the correct distance from the house down to about 12 in. Mix the concrete, and holding the post vertical, pour it around each post up to just above ground level. Check with a level that the post is both vertically and horizontally straight. Each post should be cut off so that its top finishes level with the top of the batten on the house wall. Leave the concrete to set overnight.

4 Screw a 2 × 6 in. beam (the same size as the batten on the wall) to the outside of each of the concreted posts, using two stainless-steel screws for each post. Be sure that the top of the beam finishes level with the posts, which will also mean that it finishes level with the batten on the wall (provided that the posts have been set at the correct height). This beam and the batten attached to the wall will support the deck joists.

5 Lay out the 2 × 4 in. joists from the batten on the wall to the outer beam, at even spacings of approximately 16 in. Nail the joists at both ends into the supporting beam and batten by angling two nails so that they cross each other (this is known as "cross-nailing"), but only drive them in when you are fully satisfied that the joists are correctly positioned. You will need to make sure that a joist is positioned to support each outer edge of the decking area, and this may require slight adjustments to the positions of the joists in between to keep the spacing even.

3 Once you have dug the post holes and put the posts in, pour concrete around them. Use a level to make sure that they are straight.

4 You can now screw the beams to the outside of the concreted posts. These will then support the deck joists.

5 Begin to position the deck joists in even spacings, and cross-nail them to the supporting beams.

6 With all the joists fixed into position, nail a fascia board of the same dimensions across the ends of the joists to provide a neat finish at each edge of the decking area. In this particular project, the decking boards extend beyond the fascia, but you could fix a deeper fascia board, allowing it to stand slightly above the joist by the depth of the decking boards. This will then box in the ends of the decking boards and give a crisp appearance.

7 Set out the deck boards, making sure that the boards at each end of the deck area overhang the fascia by about 1 in., which will provide a shadow line to give good definition at the edge of the deck. If the area to be decked is relatively small, you can space out all the boards to see how they fit before screwing them down. If the area is too large for this, however, just fix the boards directly and make adjustments to spacing as you near completion. Plan the layout of the boards with staggered joints, as if you were laying bricks, since this looks better than long joint lines across the whole width of the deck.

8 Space the boards with about 1/4-in. gaps between them to allow for expansion, free drainage, and air circulation. A nail knocked into a small piece of wood makes a good spacer. Use stainless-steel screws or special decking screws to fix the boards in position. Start by fixing one screw at each end to hold the board in position, and then double screw each end to firmly fix the board down. When all the decking has been completed, tidy up any cut ends by sawing and staining as necessary.

Planting ideas

On its own, the natural material of timber decking blends beautifully in a garden setting. However, you might like to further integrate a decking patio into the overall scheme of your garden by planting strategically to soften the edges, or by allowing light foliage trees to grow through cutout spaces in the deck itself. If the scale of your patio is such that cutting plant spaces would cause too much disruption to the main area, there is always the option of positioning container plants around the edge.

6 You can then use nails to fix the fascia boards to the ends of each of the joists. This will finish them off neatly.

7 The deck boards should be laid out next. You can adjust their positions until you are satisfied with their placement.

8 Use a piece of wood with a nail knocked into it as a spacer to ensure the decking boards are evenly spaced as you fix them.

maintenance
AND REPAIR

Once you have completed all of the necessary construction in your garden, it is important to make sure that the surfaces are maintained properly. If you do not repair any loose paving slabs, clean steps regularly, and properly store your tools, these features will become dangerous to all who use them. Follow the suggestions below to make sure your garden is a safe one.

Paving

If your paved surfaces have been laid properly, then they should require very little maintenance other than an occasional hosing down. All paving will inevitably accumulate dirt over a period of time, and you may welcome this for the naturally weathered appearance it will lend to the surface.

Too much dirt, however, can cause surfaces to become slippery, and this can be especially dangerous on natural stone paving that lies in shaded areas, where it will also attract algae. In this case, it is important to clean off the surface with a stiff broom and a weak solution of cleaning fluid before hosing it down. It is also a good idea to cut back any overhanging plants from such an area to expose the paving to more sunlight so it can dry out properly.

Some clay paving bricks are particularly prone to efflorescence on their surface, which is the appearance of harmless white salts. Washing the paving down will not alleviate the problem, because dampness draws the salts to the surface. Use a stiff brush (not a wire one) to remove the worst of the powdery deposits when the bricks are thoroughly dry.

Jet washes

A jet wash can work wonders bringing a surface almost back to its brand-new condition, but it is not ideal for all paved areas. The jet is so powerful that it may cause damage to the wood fibers on a timber deck, while any loose aggregates set between paving slabs will be sent flying.

A jet wash will reveal if there are any poor-quality mortar joints in your patio. If you need to repoint, then jet washing can also present you with a quick method of removing any old, crumbling mortar.

Jet washing.

Repairing weathered joints

Make sure that all of the joints are cleaned out to a good depth, about 1 in., before filling them again with a strong mortar mix. This is necessary because if your new mortar is a shallow layer, it will be quickly blown out by frost. Use a club hammer and cold chisel when you chip out the old mortar between the slabs.

Chipping out the mortar from a joint.

Replacing broken slabs

Any broken paving slabs or bricks in your patio should be removed and replaced quickly to keep anyone from tripping and injuring themselves. A slab or brick set into the middle of a terrace is far harder to replace than one on the edge of it, and you will probably need to break it out using a club hammer and bolster.

Once the slab has been removed, chip out the old mortar bed, spread a depth of new mortar in its place, and lower a new slab back into the correct position. Finish the process off by tapping the slab down firmly. This can be done by using a maul or a club hammer that is hit against a block of wood placed on the slab. After the new slab has been put in, the surrounding joints can be repointed.

Repointing around a newly laid slab.

Sand-bedded paving bricks are very straightforward to replace, which is why this type of paving is often used in urban settings where access to utility services may occasionally be required. Bricks within areas of paving that have settled can be lifted out quite easily. You might need to break out the first brick to gain access to all the others, but after that, the bricks can be removed quickly from the pattern, because there is no mortar holding them together.

Removing the first paving brick.

Once a sufficient area of bricks has been removed, dry sand can be placed and screeded out before compacting, resanding, and screeding to the correct level. The bricks are then relaid and tapped into place to provide a seamless repair.

Relaying sand-bedded bricks.

Steps

Paved steps must always be kept clean and in a good state of repair to keep them from becoming treacherous to those who use them. Slate, gravel, and bark treads may occasionally need topping up and raking out if they become worn with constant use.

If a paving slab tread is cracked or broken, it must be replaced as soon as possible, because it is very dangerous to leave it as it is. This is a simple operation if the slab is not bedded under the next riser, as you can just pry it out. However, if it is bedded under a riser, you will need to cut it out to avoid dismantling the steps. Use a slab cutter to cut through the slab as close as possible to the step riser that is holding it in, then pry up the slab and chip out the mortar bed underneath with a club hammer and bolster. Try to clean out as much old mortar as possible to make room for

Using a slab cutter to remove a slab.

a good depth of new bedding mortar.

Cut a new slab to size and lay it in position, remembering to bed it with a slight slope to the front of the step in order to shed any surface water that collects (see pages 24–5).

Maintenance of tools

Looking after tools properly will not only extend their life, but will also make the jobs for which you use them easier to carry out. Trying to lay bricks using a trowel encrusted with old mortar, for example, is frustrating, to say the least. All tools should be dried, oiled, and stored in a dry shed or garage—tools that have been used with concrete and mortar should have all excess material removed before scrubbing and washing.

Keep all your tools safe and tidy, ideally hung on the wall and not piled in a corner where it can be all too easy to trip over them. Woodworking tools, such as saws, chisels, and planes, should be covered to avoid blunting. They should also be stored in a box and kept out of the reach of young children.

As long as you are careful with your tools, the good-quality ones that you invest in now will last you a lifetime.

index

suppliers

The publishers and photographer would like to thank the following for permission to take photographs of their gardens.

(NGS: indicates a garden that is open under the National Garden Scheme.)

The Belfry Hotel, Thame, p. 113.

Sue and Jeff Brown, Adderbury, (designers: Jonathan and Amanda Ford) p. 12; p. 13 top left, bottom middle; p. 72 far left; p. 108 middle right; p. 111 top left.

Mr and Mrs Coote, Headington, pp. 38–9; p. 40 middle right; p. 111 bottom far left.

Mr and Mrs Cox, Marcliff, (NGS), p. 13 top middle, bottom left; p. 43 bottom middle left; p. 63; p. 111 bottom far right.

Mr and Mrs Evans, Bath, pp. 70–71; pp. 84–5; pp. 106–7.

Jeff and Emma Follas Decorative Landscaping, Fakenham, p. 43 top right; p. 109 bottom; p. 125.

Amanda Foster, London, pp. 6–7; p. 86 far right.

Capel Manor, Enfield, p. 43 bottom middle right, far right; p. 51 (Gardening Which Gardens); p. 75 bottom middle right; p111. bottom middle right.

Honor Gibbs, EDA Design Associates, Long Crendon, p. 99.

Heale House and Plant Centre, Middle Woodford (open to the public), p. 86 middle right; p. 88; p. 89 bottom middle right.

Mr and Mrs Hollingbery, Alresford (NGS), p. 8; p. 87 top right; p. 89 bottom middle left.

Mr and Mrs Huntingdon, Sudborough (NGS), p. 41 bottom; p. 73 bottom.

Claire and Nigel Jinks, Thurlaston, p. 81, p. 129.

Mr and Mrs Key, Fawler, p. 117.

Mrs Rani Lall, Oxford, (NGS), p. 42; p. 75 top right; p. 89 top left; p. 109 top left.

Mr and Mrs Morrison, Turweston, p. 67.

Fiona and John Owens, Chalford, p. 87 top left.

Tony Poulton, Worcester (NGS), p. 89 bottom far right.

RHS Chelsea Flower Show, p. 13 top right; p. 40 far left, far right; p. 41 top left (designer: Stephen Woodhams); p. 43 bottom far left; p. 75 bottom middle left; p. 89 top right.

RHS Hampton Court Flower Show, p. 13 bottom right; p. 40 middle left; p. 41 top right (designers: Isabelle Van Groeningen and Gabriella Pape, You Magazine); p. 43 top left (designer: World of Water); p. 72 middle left, middle right, far right; p. 73 top left (designer: Charlotte Ashburner, The Millennium Revolution), top right; p. 75 top left (designer: You Magazine), bottom far left, far right; p. 86 far left, middle left; p. 89 bottom far left; p. 108 far left, middle left, far right; p. 111 bottom middle left.

Mr and Mrs Royle, Balscote (NGS), p. 87 bottom.

Mr and Mrs Sharp, Haddenham, p. 103.

Mr and Mrs Sidaway, Twickenham (NGS), p. 109 top right; p. 111 top right.

Benjamin Smith Landscape Architect, Litchborough (NGS), p. 110.

Diana Yakeley, Yakely Associates, London (NGS), p. 95.

Yarnton Nurseries, Yarnton, p. 14 bottom right.

York Gate, Adel Nr Leeds (open to the public); Gardeners' Royal Benevolent Society, Leatherhead, pp. 4–5; p. 59.

Recommended stores where you can buy gardening supplies and equipment:

Ace Hardware
2200 Kensington Ct.
Oak Brook, IL 60523-2100
(630) 990-6600
www.acehardware.com

Gardener's Supply Company
128 Intervale Road
Burlington, VT 05401
(888) 833-1412
www.gardeners.com

Home Depot
2455 Pace Ferry Rd.
Atlanta, GA 30339
(800) 430-3376
www.homedepot.com

House 2 Home
3345 Michelson Drive
Irvine, CA 92612
(877) 980-7467
www.house2home.com

IKEA
www.ikea.com

Lowe's Home Improvement Warehouse
P.O. Box 1111
North Wilkesboro, NC 28656
(800) 44-LOWES
www.lowes.com

Restoration Hardware
15 Koch Road, Suite J
Corte Madera, CA 94925-1240
(800) 816-0969
www.restorationhardware.com

Smith & Hawken
(800) 940-1170
www.smithandhawken.com

Target
(888) 304-4000
www.target.com

acknowledgments

My thanks go to Karen Hemingway for her tireless organization and her patience. Thanks also to Juliette Wade for her superb photography, to Fay Singer for turning a book about bricks and mortar into a work of art, and to everyone who allowed us to photograph their gardens. I am also indebted to my wife, Ruthie—yet again—for everything.

A special thank you to my good friends Bernard and Gillian Davison for their hospitality and for the use of their wonderful garden. Thanks as always to Bernard for his knowledge and expertise and to his men, Chris, Alan, Bobby, and H for their hard work, craftsmanship, and sense of humor, which prevailed through many long days.

Laurel Glen Publishing
An imprint of the Advantage Publishers Group
5880 Oberlin Drive, San Diego, CA 92121-4794
www.advantagebooksonline.com

All notations of errors or omissions should be addressed to Laurel Glen Publishing, editorial department, at the above address. All other correspondence (author inquiries, permissions and rights) concerning the content of this book should be addressed to Murdoch Books U.K. Ltd., Ferry House, 51–57 Lacy Road, Putney, London, SW15 1PR, England.

ISBN 1-57145-824-7
Library of Congress Cataloging-in-Publication Data available upon request.

Printed in Singapore by Tien Wah Press

1 2 3 4 5 06 05 04 03 02

Senior Commissioning Editor: Karen Hemingway
Art Direction and Design: Fay Singer
Project Editors: Alastair Laing and Claire Musters
Managing Editor: Anna Osborn
Design Manager: Helen Taylor
Photographer: Juliette Wade
Illustrator: Nicola Gregory
Stylist: Stephanie Bateman

CEO: Robert Oerton
Publisher: Catie Ziller
Production Manager: Lucy Byrne
International Sales Director: Kevin Lagden

Color separation by Colourscan, Singapore